W9-AYZ-991

Traveler's Guide to the Firearm Laws of the Fifty States

Nineteenth Edition -- January, 2015

"Serving America's Gun Owners since 1996"

Readers should note the following changes in state firearm laws that occurred in the various state legislatures during the 2014 calendar year. These changes, along with updates to the reciprocity, contact information & traveler's checklist constitute the main differences between the 18th and 19th editions. Owners of past editions should also be aware that most state pages have been revised over the last five editions to provide more in-depth information in an easier to understand format.

Although rare, court challenges to recently passed statutes sometimes occur. Readers should stay abreast of national news so they are aware of any such challenges in the following states.

Arizona: 19-year-old military members may apply for concealed weapon licenses

California: all firearms brought into state by new residents must be registered; federal court restricts discretion of sheriffs in determining "good cause" for license issuance *(Peruta v. County of San Diego)*

District of Columbia: concealed carry-licensing law enacted

Florida: court rules that public universities may not prohibit gun possession in vehicles parked on campuses; license applications may be made to certified tax collectors

Georgia: carry options expanded for permittees, carry allowed in govt. buildings with no security screenings; preemption law strengthened

Hawaii: court rules that resident aliens may also apply for firearm acquisition permits

Idaho: enhanced permittees and retired police officers may carry firearms in certain areas of state university campuses

Illinois: vehicle carry by non-resident requires license issued by home state

Indiana: vehicle carry exception for K-12 school grounds enacted

Kansas: preemption law strengthened, local ordinances regulating vehicle carry of guns by non-permittees eliminated

Kentucky: residents may no longer use out-of-state carry licenses for in-state carry

Louisiana: licensees may carry in restaurants that serve alcohol

Massachusetts: Class "B" firearm licenses eliminated

Michigan: short barreled rifle and shotgun possession lawful under provisions of National Firearms Act

Mississippi: preemption law strengthened to provide for legal sanctions against cities that violate its provisions

Missouri: local regulation of open carry by permittees preempted; minimum age for car carry w/o permit lowered to 19; minimum age for license application lowered to 19

New York: federal court strikes down state's 7 round magazine limit

Oklahoma: licensees allowed vehicle carry of firearms when parked on K-12 school grounds

Oregon: state court defines campsite as "temporary residence" so as to qualify for unlicensed concealed carry

Pennsylvania: attorney general opinion removes prohibition on gun carry by recognized licensees in casinos; preemption law strengthened to provide legal remedy against cities violating its provisions

South Carolina: permit term increased to five years; permittees may carry in businesses that serve alcohol; carry options in vehicles expanded for permittees

Tennessee: vehicle carry of loaded firearms by non-permittees lawful; permit term increased to 5 years; parking lot storage law strengthened; firearm law preemption strengthened

Utah: disorderly conduct charges prohibited against persons who open carry

Washington: short barreled rifle possession lawful under provisions of National Firearms Act

West Virginia: preemption law strengthened, grandfather clause removed; gun possession in the field during hunting season does not necessarily indicate illegality

Traveler's Guide
P.O. Box 2156
Covington, KY 41012
(859) 491-6400

www.gunlawguide.com

How to Use this Guide

The wide variety of firearm laws facing the gun owner of the early twenty-first century can be very intimidating when traveling outside one's own state. Many horror stories exist in which the nonresident traveler is arrested on a firearm felony charge for a violation that wouldn't qualify as a misdemeanor in the traveler's home state. A routine traffic stop suddenly degenerates into a nightmare journey through the criminal justice system. The unsuspecting traveler is hauled off to jail and forced to await the intervention of an attorney while his vehicle is searched and later impounded.

One story, which typifies the humiliation of such a situation, occurred several years ago on the New Jersey turnpike. A businessman from North Carolina was traveling to Maine via New Jersey when he was stopped by a New Jersey State trooper for a speeding violation. During the routine questioning, the trooper asked the North Carolina man if he had any firearms in the vehicle. Having a concealed carry permit from North Carolina, the traveler assumed he was operating well within the law. He told the trooper that he had a Glock 19 semi-automatic pistol in his briefcase that he was licensed to carry and would be more than happy to allow the trooper to inspect it. Before the traveler could utter another word, the trooper had drawn his sidearm, pointed it at the traveler and began shouting at the man to exit the vehicle at once with his hands in the air. The stunned businessman, who had never had so much as a parking ticket, did as the officer demanded. He soon found himself spread eagle on the ground while the agitated trooper called for assistance. In the days after his arrest, the traveler was charged with a felony and spent three days in a Newark jail. He was eventually placed in a diversion program while the felony charge was pled down to a misdemeanor. But if the traveler had not possessed such an exemplary prior record, he may have faced the original felony and prison time. In traveling through New Jersey, the traveler failed to take into account the radical difference in legal firearms carry from his native state of North Carolina. Such a lapse could have cost him much more than it did.

This guide will prevent the occurrence of such an incident by providing the traveler with an outline of the legal pitfalls he may encounter while carrying his firearms from state to state. Beginning with Alabama and continuing in alphabetical order through Wyoming, each state is afforded one page of explanation pertaining to the firearm laws most relevant to the traveler. The District of Columbia, Canada and Mexico are also covered. A bar graph showing how each state is rated for its treatment of firearms is displayed in the top margin of each page. Any change in firearms freedom from the previous year is noted as well as the reason behind the change. When no change has occurred, the author provides the reader with a short phrase summarizing why the state has its current rating. This provides a quick reference when time is of the essence. Vehicle carry of firearms, concealed carry and reciprocity for non-resident licensees, and laws governing possession of all firearm types are covered in a user friendly format for each state.

Shall Issue vs. May Issue

The reader will find the terms "shall issue" and "may issue" used extensively throughout this Guide. "Shall issue" refers to the statutory language in states where the issuance of a license to carry concealed is not dependent upon the discretion of a local law enforcement officer. If an applicant satisfies a number of objective criteria (ie. no felony record, no record of mental defect, etc.) and completes whatever training course is mandated by the law, the applicant *must* be issued a license regardless of what the issuing authority personally thinks of the individual. Most states with concealed carry laws operate their licensing procedure in this manner.

"May issue" refers to states that allow a certain amount of discretion over the issuance of a permit to carry a firearm. The local sheriff may require that the applicant demonstrate a viable need to carry a weapon by showing that the applicant has had his life threatened recently or requires a gun because of his current occupation. Fortunately for gun owners, "may issue" states are rapidly becoming an endangered minority. The recent flurry of interest in concealed carry laws has forced most states that formerly had discretionary issuance to amend their laws to make them "shall issue."

Reciprocity and Recognition

The traveler's concern with the concealed carry law of the various states is rooted in the issue of reciprocity. Many states with concealed carry licensing laws will recognize the out-of-state carry permits of travelers under certain conditions. Some of these states provide universal or "automatic" recognition for any foreign state's permits. These states will recognize any valid, out-of-state permit to carry a firearm regardless of bureaucratic interpretation. Other states will qualify their recognition of a foreign state's permits on the foreign state recognizing the permits of the host state or having issuance standards which are similar to the standards of the host state. Recognition of permits in these states is often at the discretion of the attorney general or state police. Such discretion indicates the potential for inconsistency. Travelers journeying to these states should verify the status of their out-of-state permits if they intend to use their permits for firearms carry. An up-to-date list is provided on p. 65 with the reciprocity status of the conditional states at the time of printing. Travelers may also further confirm the status of the states they are visiting by contacting any one of the official state agencies listed on p. 62. Some states modify their reciprocity lists without warning. So verification is always a good idea. Readers of the print version may use the map (p.9) to color code the states where their permits are recognized. This will make for convenient quick reference.

An issue that is fast becoming a problem for travelers is that of non-resident permits. More and more states are issuing permits to persons who are not residents of the issuing state. And some states that do not issue permits to nonresidents will make special exception for military personnel stationed in the state. This has been of immense benefit to citizens living in restrictive states such as New Jersey and New York who sometimes find it almost impossible to acquire in-state permits. But the downside has been a number of states that are refusing to recognize out-of-state permits that are issued to persons who are not residents of the issuing state. Various justifications are given as to why this is being done. None of these explanations really answer the question as to why a non-resident, who passes through the same background checks as a resident, is less qualified for recognition than a resident. The bottom line for the traveler is that this can be a sticky wicket. While using this Guide to check the recognition status of your permit, be sure to note which states do not honor non-resident permits. These states are set apart on p.65-67 with a star (*). States that do not recognize out-of-state permits held by their own residents are underlined on those same pages. A more detailed explanation regarding this issue is provided on each state page.

When carrying concealed outside of one's vehicle in a state that provides reciprocity, the traveler carries subject to the restrictions imposed on concealed carry in that state. Most states only issue licenses for handgun carry. Therefore, travelers should only use their permits to carry handguns unless they are sure that the state they are visiting allows other weapons to be carried with a permit. The individual should have immediate possession of his carry permit and watch for postings that prohibit carry in certain areas, such as public parks and government buildings, by permittees. If approached by a police officer for a law enforcement purpose, the permittee should notify the officer that he has a permit to carry a concealed weapon and the firearm is present on his person. This action may not be legally required in all states. But it is prudent in order to avoid any misunderstanding on the part of the officer as to one's status as a law-abiding citizen.

Concealed vs. Plain View

Related to the issue of licensing are the actual definitions of the terms "concealed" and "plain view." The meaning of these terms might vary from state to state depending on how the statutes and case law of a particular state define them. Generally, however, concealed includes readily accessible firearms that are "hidden from ordinary observation on or about one's person." While in a vehicle, this definition would almost always include under one's outer clothing or in a closed container such as a purse or gym bag that is actually carried by the person. Many states also regard having a hidden firearm within arms reach to be carrying concealed. This would include glove compartment, console box and seat pocket containment.

Plain view usually refers to firearms that are visible from a vantage point outside the vehicle.

This carry mode is utilized primarily while the vehicle is occupied and the owner wishes to have immediate access to his firearms for personal defense. In a holster or sling while on the vehicle's dashboard, passenger's seat or gun rack is considered acceptable in most states that mandate plain view carry. Travelers carrying firearms in plain view may find it prudent to secure their weapons in a trunk or rear storage area when they are not occupying the vehicle. All states which allow plain view passenger compartment carry allow cased and unloaded trunk transport as well.

"Traveler's Checklist" Terms Defined

In the "Travelers Checklist," the phrase *"standard firearm ownership"* refers to legal title of "non-military pattern" handguns & long guns and not to carry, transportation, or purchase. Some states will not permit mere ownership of certain firearms without an identification card and go as far as to require a license to simply possess a firearm in your own home. These licenses are usually subject to renewal every few years and may be revoked by authorities for any number of reasons.

The section entitled *"Vehicle Carry for non-permittees"* refers to vehicle carry by persons *without* recognized permits. Most states allow persons with recognized permits to carry handguns anywhere in the vehicle. Specific exceptions are noted in the text. Those persons who do not have permits must follow certain statutory rules for vehicle carry. This section examines these rules.

The term *posted* is used repeatedly in the text and simply refers to businesses or other entities that may post signs prohibiting firearms carry on their premises.

The terms *permittee* and *non-permittee* are used throughout the Guide. Generally, a permittee is a person who possesses a carry permit that is recognized in the state being discussed. A non-permittee is a person who does not possess a recognized permit in that state. Also, the terms "license" and "permit" are used interchangeably throughout the text.

Glove compartment and *vehicle storage compartment* are two terms that are not interchangeable. Vehicle storage compartment refers to a storage area that is located outside the passenger compartment and requires one to exit the vehicle in order to access it. Glove compartment refers to the factory-installed compartment located in front of a vehicle's passenger seat. Console boxes and seat pockets are not glove compartments.

Securely encased refers to firearms that are placed in closed commercial gun cases which are latched, but not necessarily locked, in place. "Securely encased" does not include the carry of a firearm in a case not designed to hold a gun. Purses, gym bags and briefcases would not qualify as securely encased containers. But hard plastic cases manufactured specifically for firearm containment would be legitimate.

State Parks is a section that covers the issue of carry by recognized permittees. Many states have carved out exceptions to general gun prohibitions for licensees but still prohibit open carry by non-licensees. As a rule, if a state allows concealed carry by permittees, it will also allow non-permittees to keep their firearms cased and unloaded in their vehicles. Many states may also allow handgun carry by permittees but will require long guns carried by anyone to be unloaded and cased.

Restaurants serving alcohol is a section that is limited to specific parameters. Restaurants are eating establishments such as Applebees or Fridays that serve alcohol but produce most of their income from the sale of food. The term would not include "Joe's Corner Bar" that may serve pizzas and pretzels but is primarily a "watering hole" for those wishing to imbibe. If the Guide indicates that recognized permittees can carry in restaurants it means that permittees can carry concealed, loaded handguns if they do not consume alcohol, remain in the dining area and do not frequent the "bar portion" of the establishment. Granted, some states may allow permittees to drink and visit the bars of these restaurants, but enough states limit this privilege to make these guidelines necessary. Most states that allow carry in these restaurants allow businesses to post signs against such carry. Do not be surprised if you see some restaurants in "carry friendly" states posted against carry.

Duty to Notify LEO of permit status refers to the permit holder's duty to notify an approaching *Law Enforcement Officer (LEO)* that he has a concealed weapon and a license authorizing him to carry it. States will either require "immediate notification" upon initial contact with the officer or notification upon officer request. The states that require *immediate notification* put the burden on the licensee to tell the officer that he has a permit with a concealed weapon. Failure to immediately do so upon first contact can result in an arrest. So be especially careful in these states.

Right of Self-defense

The "Right of Self-defense" section in the Traveler's checklist indicates how each state protects a traveler's self-defense rights. It references whether a state has enacted an "NRA-model castle doctrine" in the last ten years and whether a citizen has a right to "stand his ground" in public areas and not retreat when threatened with deadly force. Most states have some form of the "common law castle doctrine" which provides *stand your ground* rights in your home. But many of the "NRA-model castle doctrines" extend this right to public areas outside one's home. Most reference any place "where a person has a right to be." Others limit the right to your vehicle. Some states may have "stand your ground" language in their case law but have not "codified" or "written it into" their statutes. These states are noted as being "not codified."

The section is not intended to provide the reader with in-depth knowledge of a state's self-defense laws. Rather it is meant to act as a barometer for the casual traveler in assessing a state's attitude toward self-defense rights outside of one's home. Too often, citizens who use deadly force to defend themselves are subsequently prosecuted by over-zealous district attorneys and even sued in civil court by their attackers. The result is a chilling effect. A citizen is afraid to use a gun for self-defense for fear of being turned into a criminal. This section will allow the traveler to determine which states are friendly to the citizen and which ones coddle the criminal.

Vehicle Gun Possession at Colleges

Most colleges and universities prohibit firearms carry in buildings and campus facilities. But some states have begun to carve out exceptions for gun possession in vehicles located on campus parking lots. The Guide provides an overview of this by classifying the regulatory action each state undertakes. Some states prohibit all gun possession on college campuses (vehicles included) through their criminal or administrative codes. Violating these rules could result in criminal sanctions such as arrest and prosecution. Other states allow each college to determine regulatory action through policy. Those connected in some way to the college (students, faculty and staff) are most at risk. They can be fired, expelled or face civil sanctions. Aside from muted trespass charges, not much can be done to penalize the occasional visitor. A small but growing number of states exempt those holding valid carry licenses from criminal action and, in some cases, also exempt all lawful gun owners. Perhaps the safest states are the ones such as Kentucky, which, along with exempting all gun owners from criminal sanctions, also prevent colleges from restricting vehicle gun possession through policy.

The Guide classifies each state based on these regulatory schemes. Readers should note that where vehicle gun possession is allowed, the firearm should remain locked in one's vehicle and hidden from view. If the state only exempts permittees, then only the weapons that one may carry with a valid permit (ie handguns) may be stored in the vehicle.

Some states exempt gun owners from criminal sanctions but allow the enforcement of college policy that could adversely affect those connected with the institution. These states are noted appropriately under each subheading. And readers should not be surprised to see "no gun" signs in campus parking lots where possession of lawful firearms is allowed. Some colleges still attempt to enforce "no gun" policies in spite of state laws that prevent such rules; proving that academics will often bend the rules to meet their own ideological ends.

Loaded vs. Unloaded

The term "loaded" refers to firearms that have live ammunition in either the magazine or the chamber. A firearm with any number of rounds in its magazine is considered loaded under the laws of most states even if no live round is in the chamber. The three notable exceptions to this general rule are Colorado, Nevada and Utah which define "loaded" as only applying to firearms with a live round in the chamber. Some states consider guns that are in close proximity to magazines containing ammunition to be "loaded." Other states prohibit magazines from being inserted into firearms but allow loaded magazines to be located within arms reach of the firearm. These state-by-state differences are noted appropriately within the text.

Travelers should also keep all loaded firearms out of reach of their children while in a vehicle. A small number of states criminalize those who keep firearms in any place where a child might access the weapon. Some states, such as Ohio and Colorado, have specific laws in this regard. Other states may attempt enforcement through generalized laws involving child endangerment.

Open Carry

The open carry status of a state is another aspect covered in the Traveler's Checklist that may require some prefacing. Carrying a handgun that is unconcealed on your person is a way for some persons to carry who do not have the benefit of a recognized concealed carry permit. Many states do not criminalize such behavior; thus making this mode of carry legitimate under law. But travelers should use common sense when attempting open carry in heavily populated urban areas where such carry is not widespread. Even in states that allow such carry in theory, police may stop and question an individual who is displaying a firearm on his hip for all to see. Granted, no person who is exercising a fundamental right should have to worry about being harassed for otherwise legal behavior. But such scrutiny can and does occur in the real world. A traveler should simply exercise good judgment and keep his handgun secured in a snapped, visible belt holster.

Interstate transport through restrictive states

Readers will also notice occasional references to the McClure-Volkmer Act of 1986 and its specific treatment of interstate firearms transport. This federal law is listed in the U.S. Code as an amendment to the Gun Control Act of 1968. It serves to correct certain draconian aspects of the 1968 law as well as make interstate transport of firearms less restrictive. Persons transporting firearms through a state that would otherwise view such transport as illegal may do so if the weapons are unloaded, cased and stowed in a trunk or vehicle storage compartment which is not readily accessible to the occupants. Any ammunition must also be kept separate from the firearms. Persons operating vehicles without trunks or external storage compartments may transport unloaded firearms in "locked" cases. Internal storage compartments other than console boxes or glove compartments that are locked may also suffice when a trunk is not available.

The traveler must simply be passing through the state and must be bound for a jurisdiction where possession of such weapons is legal. Any extended stops for reasons other than gas or emergency services would effectively nullify the traveler's interstate commerce classification and subject him to the effects of state law. For example, a traveler from Kentucky bound for Maine with Class III machine guns will pass through the state of New York. New York does not permit individual possession of machine guns. As long the traveler maintains a steady, uninterrupted course through the state with the offending weapons stowed in the manner described above, he is operating within the parameters of federal law. As soon as the traveler stops to visit relatives in Albany, he falls within the police power of New York. He could be arrested for possessing firearms that are illegal under New York law. Some travelers have found it beneficial to have a hotel or campground pre-registration form with them when trekking through restrictive states such as New York. This form proves to any state trooper that you are actually traveling to a legitimate, gun-friendly destination and have no intention of remaining within the restrictive state for an extended period.

The Code only references firearms or ammunition. So the law *may* not cover a box of high capacity magazines (or other component parts) that are prohibited in a restrictive state. The courts have yet to "flesh out" the details of this aspect..

Traffic Stops

Any traveler carrying firearms should be aware of the proper way to handle a routine traffic stop. One involved in frequent travel will eventually be pulled over for a speeding violation or some other minor infraction. A motorist should avoid any erratic physical movements during a traffic stop. Both hands should remain on the steering wheel while the driver remains seated in the vehicle waiting for the officer to approach. At this point, the investigating officer has the right to ask questions of the motorist concerning his operation of the vehicle. Questions which may elicit self-incriminating information from the traveler may be refuted by simply informing the officer that the traveler would prefer to be represented by proper counsel before answering the posed question. Some officers may wish to go beyond mere questioning and conduct a search of the vehicle for contraband that could include firearms in some states. For an officer to conduct a legitimate search of a vehicle, he must have "probable cause." Most traffic stops do not provide the officer with enough probable cause for a search. Therefore, the officer will often politely ask the motorist for voluntary consent. Many citizens, fearing they will look guilty upon refusal, willingly sign the consent form the officer provides them. This is not a recommended course of action. Voluntary consent gives the officer free reign to do what he likes and nullifies any subsequent legal challenges. If asked to consent to a vehicle search, politely refuse and inform the officer that he will have to search on his own. Most officers who are unable to establish probable cause will not search without a consent form.

Travelers should note that a police officer might conduct a "protective search" of your person for weapons without probable cause. An officer may ask a motorist who appears suspicious to exit the vehicle so as to allow a frisk of the person's clothing for concealed weapons. The officer may also check the area of the vehicle under the motorist's immediate control for weapons before allowing him to reenter the vehicle. The courts allow this type of search only if the officer can articulate a reasonable suspicion that the motorist may have an illegal weapon. Such a protective search may not extend to other areas of the vehicle without probable cause of criminal activity.

Permittees sometimes wonder whether they should volunteer to an officer that they have a recognized permit if the officer does not ask. Most states do not require a citizen to divulge that information unless the officer requests it. But some states require the permittee to volunteer the information as soon as he is approached by a police officer. The states that require this action are noted in the text. As a general rule, it is recommended that no matter what the legal restriction, a recognized permittee should let an officer know that he has a permit with a gun on his person. Such notification will help avoid any escalation of what is already a tense situation. This notification is generally limited to permittees who carry under the authority of a permit. Firearms that are cased and unloaded in the trunk or storage area need not be declared unless a vehicle search is executed.

Also, recent reports indicate that police in anti-gun states such as Maryland are using license plate reader cameras to pull over gun owners from other states and search them for weapons. One family from Florida recently had their car emptied of all possessions, the husband handcuffed and the wife and kids searched because the Maryland trooper had information obtained from one of these cameras that the motorist had a carry license in his native state of Florida. The trooper claimed this gave him "probable cause" to harass the otherwise innocent family for almost two hours. Whether this is standard policy in Maryland has yet to be determined. But, be advised, this case illustrates how police in other states may know your license status before they even pull you over.

Universally Restricted Areas

Firearms carry is universally prohibited in certain areas even with a concealed carry permit. Federal installations such as Post Offices (including parking lots), courthouses and administrative offices and some federal management areas such as Corp of Engineer properties forbid gun carry inside buildings and, in most instances, on the outside premises. Military bases prohibit firearms carry by visitors and also restrict firearm possession within one's vehicle. Search and seizure rules on military property are more liberally construed than elsewhere. Visitors and military personnel should check with officials before visiting a military installation with firearms.

Most states prohibit firearms carry within preschool, primary & secondary schools (K-12). Harsh penalties are usually set for violating this restriction. Federal law prohibits firearm possession within 1000 ft. of primary and secondary school properties. Concealed weapon permittees from the state in which the school is located, persons possessing unloaded firearms in locked containers inside their vehicles and private property areas within the zone are exempt from this prohibition.

Firearms carry is also prohibited in law enforcement offices, detention facilities, courthouses, legislative meetings, polling booths and public buildings that house governmental offices where official business is conducted. Many states also prohibit firearms in mental health and day care facilities as well as retail establishments whose **primary** business is the sale of alcohol by the drink (bars). Exceptions to these general rules do exist. But, for the most part, travelers should consider these areas to be off-limits unless the Guide states otherwise.

National Parks, Forests and Indian Reservations

Firearm possession in National Parks and wildlife refuges is governed by 16 USC section 1a-7b of the U.S. Code. This 2010 change mandates that firearm possession and carry in these areas is regulated by the state where the park or refuge is located. For example, if your permit is recognized in Idaho, you can carry in any park or refuge located in Idaho, subject to the carry restrictions of Idaho. This expansion of the right to carry only applies to outdoor areas such as nature trails and campsites. All official structures such as visitor centers and ranger stations are still off-limits to any gun carry. Private vendors with gift shops and restaurants are not automatically off-limits. But most states allow these entities to post signs that prohibit carry.

National Forests are under the management of the Department of Agriculture and are not subject to the same regulatory action as National Parks. The law of the state where the National Forest is located is usually the law that prevails for gun carry. If a state allows open carry, the National Forests in that state also allow open carry unless otherwise posted. Some travelers have reported "no firearms" signs in National Forests that are located in otherwise firearms-friendly states. These signs may exist because a state's law specifically prohibits carry in a national forest. Or the signs may be posted by officials attempting to enforce an otherwise unenforceable policy. Either way, travelers should know that authorities may enforce these restrictions regardless of their legal basis.

Indian reservations *may have* stricter firearm carry laws within their boundaries than the states where they are located. This condition exists because reservations are relatively autonomous areas that exist as quasi-independent nations. It is beyond the scope of this Guide to cover each reservation specifically. But travelers visiting casinos and other tourist attractions inside reservations would be well-advised to transport all firearms in an unloaded, cased and secure manner that is consistent with the McClure-Volkmer Act discussed earlier. Carry of firearms on one's person is not recommended unless the traveler verifies with the tribal council that such action is lawful.

Motorcycle Issues

Motorcycle riders often ask how carry laws written for four-wheel vehicles apply to them. For example, where is the glove compartment in a motorcycle? Does a saddlebag qualify as a legitimate container for gun carry? Most states' laws do not specifically address these issues. So definitive answers are difficult. But motorcycle owners can follow some general rules and be sure of compliance in most states.

The rear compartment on a motorcycle qualifies as a trunk if it contains a lock. An unloaded handgun in this locked compartment should be legitimate in most states that prohibit loaded firearms in a vehicle. And, of course, a carry permit would allow the concealed carry of a loaded firearm on one's person in states that recognize the permit. Tote bags have the same effect as a briefcase or gym bag carried on a vehicle's front seat. Most weapons in this venue would be considered concealed.

If one lacks a recognized permit while visiting a state that allows open carry, a firearm could be carried in a hip holster in plain view. This carry mode might appear somewhat aggressive to other motorists and could result in unnecessary attention from police. But it would be an otherwise legal way to carry a handgun in a state that allows open carry. A motorist would have to weigh the advantage of being legally armed with the disadvantage of being subject to increased scrutiny.

Motorhome and RV issues

A common question among RV owners is whether their motorhomes are considered vehicles or residences. Most states consider RVs to be readily mobile and thus subject to all firearm laws concerning vehicular travel. But courts have held that RVs in a fixed state (ie. in a designated campground and hooked up to water, sewer, electric and other utilities) are residences. RV owners should keep this in mind so as to be aware of what their classification is at any one particular time. Many states will allow loaded firearms possession in one's home while prohibiting it in one's vehicle.

Occasional references are made to the trunk transport of firearms. The usual response from RV owners is, "I drive an RV, I don't have a trunk." Most state statutes do not directly address the issue of carry within motorhomes. Because of this lack of specific reference, RV owners should think of their external compartments as having the same legal status as a standard vehicle's trunk. A trunk is generally seen as a compartment that requires one to exit the vehicle in order to gain access to it. If a recommendation is made to transport firearms in one's trunk, RVers should take this to mean that transport in a locked, external compartment is legitimate.

The same standard can be applied to trailers. These attachments require one to exit the towing vehicle to access their interiors. Transporting firearms in a trailer would have the same legal effect as transporting firearms in a trunk. Both are separate from the passenger section of the vehicle and would qualify as legitimate storage areas.

Owners of full size RVs sometimes find it difficult to apply the principle of "plain view" carry to their rigs. If the cab is extremely high, how does an approaching police officer see the gun from outside the vehicle? Simply put, the officer cannot. And if the gun is not visible from outside the vehicle, then it is not in plain view. Owners of these motorhomes must exercise another carry option if they wish to keep a loaded gun up front. Many states are allowing console box and glove compartment carry for non-permittees. These options do not have a visibility requirement and probably serve the owners of large motorhomes better than the plain view carry.

Traveling by Air, Cruise Ship, Train & Greyhound Bus

While firearm possession in the sterile areas of airports is prohibited, individuals traveling by air may transport unloaded firearms in their checked baggage. Firearms must be unloaded and secured in locked, hard-sided gun cases. Ammunition should be contained in commercial boxes and not loaded into any extraneous magazines. Firearms and ammunition may be kept in the same locked case unless a specific airline's regulations mandate otherwise. Travelers must notify their airline about the presence of the firearms and/or ammunition when checking the baggage and provide the key to their gun cases if a search is requested. Check-in procedures vary among airlines. Travelers should call ahead to verify where to check-in and what paperwork needs to be completed. Federal law now prevents airlines from marking cases containing firearms with visible "firearm" signs. If an airline employee attempts to do this, he is violating the law and should be reported to a supervisor.

A federal court recently held that the interstate transportation protections of McClure-Volkmer (p.5) only apply to vehicular travel. Travelers with connecting flights through restrictive states could face local prosecution if they possess any firearms that are illegal in those states.

Gun owners traveling by train, cruise ship, greyhound bus or other form of common carrier involved in interstate transportation must turn over possession of their legally owned firearms and ammunition to the captain, conductor or pilot of the vessel for the duration of the trip. Certain carriers will make provisions for passengers transporting firearms. But travelers are encouraged to contact the carrier before making passage to determine what that policy might be.

Over the Road Commercial Trucks

Mark Twain once said, "a rumor is half way around the world before the truth gets its boots on." One of the most often heard rumors is that federal law prohibits carrying firearms in commercial vehicles such as semi-tractor trailers. This myth has been repeated by trucking company supervisors and corporate management for years with no legal citation or statutory proof offered for support. The truth is that while many companies have internal policies that prohibit guns in company vehicles, no federal law exists that regulates guns in trucks. Truckers can carry subject to the same state and local restrictions as everyone else. Independent truckers will have an easier time carrying simply because they are not beholden to company polices that may prohibit such activity. But any trucker, regardless of company policy, ***will not*** be violating federal law if he carries a gun for personal protection.

Current & Retired Law Enforcement Officers

Federal legislation signed into effect in July 2004 allows all active duty law enforcement officers from any state or locality to carry concealed firearms while traveling. The officer must possess an official photographic identification from his department and be authorized to carry a firearm by the agency with which he is employed. The firearm may be carried in most public areas but must remain concealed. This allowance for carry does not extend to governmental or private property where a state has prohibited all firearms carry.

Retired law enforcement officers were also granted the right to carry concealed firearms while traveling in the same manner stated above. But the restrictions on their qualifying status are much greater. To be considered a "retired law enforcement officer," one must have been employed as a law enforcement officer for at least 10 years and been authorized during that period to carry a firearm and conduct arrests and investigations. If an officer did not achieve a full 10 years of service, but separated from employment early because of a service connected disability, then any probationary service period as determined by his department of employment would be acceptable. Most importantly, every retired officer must meet his state's firearms training and qualification standards for police officers every 12 months and be issued a photographic identification by the department from which he retired certifying that he has met these qualifications. A retired officer may receive certification through either the agency he retired from or any certified firearms instructor or law enforcement agency in his current state of residence.

Preemption of Local Laws

Most state legislatures have enacted statutes known as firearm preemption laws. These laws prevent cities and counties from passing ordinances that regulate the carry, possession and ownership of firearms. Some of these acts mandate total uniformity in firearm laws by prohibiting any amount of home rule while others allow local ordinances existing before the passage of the law to remain in effect. A small minority allow the local enactment of new firearm laws if the state assembly concurs. These distinctions are noted in the explanations for each state and help the traveler to determine if issues such as open carry or glove compartment placement are subject to local control. Travelers will find their journeys much easier to plan in states with comprehensive preemption laws in place.

The author of this guide hopes readers will benefit from the information discussed in the proceeding pages. Travel with firearms in the United States is as much a necessity as a guaranteed right. Knowing how to carry your firearms in a legally correct manner is as essential to safe, efficient travel as a good road atlas.

Use a colored pencil to shade the states where your permit is recognized

Alabama

Total prohibition   *(+0, good state, but still tough for vehicle carry w/o license)* **Total freedom**

0 ------ 10 ------ 20 ------ 30 ------ 40 ------ 50 ------ 60 ------ 70 ------ 80 ------ 90 ------ 100

人

Traveler's checklist:

*   ***Standard firearms ownership:** unrestricted, no permit or license required
*   ***Semi-auto / high capacity magazines:** no restrictions on possession or sale
*   ***Machine gun ownership:** no state restrictions, compliance with federal law only
*   ***Firearm law uniformity:** uniform throughout state, local units prohibited from enforcing ordinances regulating firearms; local unit liability for non-compliance
*   ***Right of Self-Defense:** NRA-model castle doctrine, *stand your ground* in public areas
*   ***Open carry:** unrestricted in most public areas; some exceptions, see below
*   ***Concealed carry:** licenses issued by county sheriffs on a shall issue basis; automatic recognition for nonresidents with carry permits from other states
*   ***Vehicle carry by non-permittees:** handguns must be unloaded and cased in the trunk or storage area unless one has a recognized permit; loaded long guns may be carried in plain view or gun cases (some exceptions, see below)
*   ***State Parks:** concealed handgun carry by recognized licensees permitted
*   ***Restaurants serving alcohol:** permittees may carry while eating in dining areas – see p.3
*   ***Duty to notify LEO of permit status:** upon demand of police officer
*   ***Vehicle gun possession at colleges:** subject to college administrative policy

Alabama's reputation as the "Heart of Dixie" is well earned when it comes to the state's strong and vibrant gun culture. Visitors will find its gun laws stricter than some other states of the Cotton Belt but generally conducive to unmolested travel.

Recognized permittees: A license is required to carry a handgun in a vehicle or concealed on or about one's person. A resident's local sheriff issues such licenses on a "shall issue" basis for one to five year terms. Alabama does not issue permits to nonresidents but will recognize any out-of-state carry permit so long as the permittee is a nonresident.

A recognized licensee may carry a loaded, concealed handgun in most public areas. Alabama is one the few states that allows its resident licensees to carry on K-12 school grounds. But, despite this relative freedom, licensees should still watch for postings that prohibit carry in certain public buildings, some universally restricted areas (p.6) and restricted access facilities.

Persons without recognized permits: A non-permittee may not carry a loaded, readily accessible handgun in a vehicle or concealed on or about his person. This would include placing a handgun under one's coat as well as hiding the weapon in a purse, briefcase or gym bag. While traveling in a vehicle, all handguns should be unloaded, cased and secured in the trunk or rear storage area. Glove compartment, console box and "under the seat" carry are not allowed.

All Persons: Loaded long guns may be transported in vehicles throughout most of the state. But certain areas, such as state parks, state land division properties and wildlife management areas, require all long guns in vehicles to be unloaded. .

Anyone may openly carry a loaded handgun while on foot in most public areas. Local units may not regulate this and most other aspects of firearm carry. But be aware that Alabama prohibits all persons from carrying firearms at or near public demonstrations. Buildings with restricted access (turnstiles, metal detectors, etc.) are also prohibited. But these places must post signs and may not prohibit possession in parked cars. Athletic events are O.K. for permittees unless the facilities are posted as "restricted access" areas. Then the prohibition applies to all.

Alaska

Total prohibition *(+0, America's frontier, great for guns, need we say more)* **Total freedom**

0 ------ 10 ------ 20 ------ 30 ------ 40 ------ 50 ------ 60 ------ 70 ------ 80 ------ 90 ------ 100

                                              λ

Traveler's checklist:

- ***Standard firearms ownership:** unrestricted, no permit or license required
- ***Semi-auto / high capacity magazines:** no restrictions on possession or sale
- ***Machine gun ownership:** no state restrictions, compliance with federal law only
- ***Firearm law uniformity:** preemption statute, localities prohibited from regulating any aspect of firearms possession and carry
- ***Right of Self-Defense:** NRA model castle doctrine, *stand your ground* in public areas
- ***Open carry:** unrestricted under state law, generally accepted in most areas
- ***Concealed carry:** licenses granted on a "shall issue" basis; automatic recognition of carry permits from all other states (see below)
- ***Vehicle carry by non-permittees:** loaded, concealed firearms may be carried anywhere in a vehicle by persons 21 years or older
- ***State Parks:** any non-felon may carry a firearm for self-defense
- ***Restaurant serving alcohol:** permittees may carry while eating in dining areas – see p.3
- ***Duty to notify LEO of permit/carry status:** immediately upon official contact
- ***Vehicle gun possession at colleges:** lawful for any gun owner

The Alaskan frontier remains a permanent part of life for most of the population. This condition makes gun ownership a popular pursuit for the state's nearly 700,000 residents. Travelers to our northern boundary will experience few problems cruising the state's tundra.

Recognized permittees: Alaska grants concealed carry permits to residents on a "shall issue" basis and recognizes permits issued by any other state or locality. A permit is issued for a five-year term and authorizes the holder to carry a loaded, concealed handgun in most public areas. The need for a permit was recently diminished when the state adopted a Vermont-style carry policy that allows any person 21 years or older to carry a concealed handgun without a license. Licenses are still issued so Alaskans can enjoy reciprocal privileges while traveling.

Persons without recognized permits: Any person who is 21 years or older may carry a concealed, loaded handgun in the passenger compartment of his vehicle or in most public areas while on foot. This allowance extends to a handgun concealed under one's coat or in a gym bag, purse or briefcase carried by the person. While in a vehicle, console box, glove compartment and "under the seat" placement are also legitimate.

All Persons: Firearms carry is prohibited in bars, schools, day care centers and private residences of others. But a traveler who is not otherwise prohibited from possessing firearms may carry a concealed handgun in a restaurant as long as he does not consume any liquor. Any person carrying a concealed firearm must always inform a police officer who contacts that person for an official purpose that he is armed with a concealed weapon.

Loaded rifles and shotguns may be carried concealed or openly while on foot or in a vehicle. Gun racks and gun cases are the most common methods of stowage in vehicles.

Local regulation of firearm issues is prohibited. Alaska recently enacted a comprehensive preemption statute that prohibits localities from regulating any aspect of firearm carry, transportation, ownership, or possession. Private businesses are also prevented from regulating firearm possession in vehicles parked on their premises. This aspect, coupled with the unrestrictive carry laws noted above, makes Alaska one of America's most gun-friendly states.

Arizona

Total prohibition   *(+0, constitutional carry and laws like the Old West)*   **Total freedom**

0 ------ 10 ------ 20 ------ 30 ------ 40 ------ 50 ------ 60 ------ 70 ------ 80 ------ 90 ------ 100

Λ

Traveler's checklist:

* **Standard firearms ownership:** unrestricted, no permit or license required
* **Semi-auto / high capacity magazines:** no restrictions on possession or sale
* **Machine gun ownership:** no state restrictions, compliance with federal law only
* **Firearm law uniformity:** local units prohibited from enacting or enforcing laws regulating most forms of firearms carry (see below)
* **Right of Self-Defense:** NRA-model castle doctrine, *stand your ground* in public areas
* **Open carry:** unrestricted under state law in most public areas and generally accepted
* **Concealed carry:** licenses granted to qualified U.S. citizens on a shall issue basis; automatic recognition of carry permits from all other states
* **Vehicle carry by non-permittees:** loaded firearms may be carried either concealed or openly by anyone who is law-abiding and 21 years or older
* **State Parks:** concealed handgun carry by recognized licensees permitted
* **Restaurants serving alcohol:** permittees may carry while eating in dining areas – see p.3
* **Duty to notify LEO of permit status:** upon demand of police officer
* **Vehicle gun possession at colleges:** lawful for any gun owner

It is not uncommon to see citizens walking the streets of major Arizona cities with holstered, loaded firearms. While this mode of carry may be legal in other states as well, open carry of a firearm without a license is perhaps more commonly practiced in the Grand Canyon State than elsewhere. The state recently extended this right to carry without a permit to include concealed carry. Arizona is now with Vermont, Wyoming and Alaska as being one of four "constitutional carry" states where citizens need not obtain permits to carry concealed weapons.

Recognized permittees: Despite acknowledging the right of "unlicensed" concealed carry, Arizona still issues licenses to carry concealed weapons on a "shall issue" basis to Arizona residents or any qualified U.S. citizen for five-year terms. Arizona recognizes any other state's permit so long as the permittee is legally present in the state, has physical possession of his license and is at least 21 years of age with no outstanding indictments or warrants.

The advantage of having a permit is that it allows persons to carry concealed weapons in some areas that are still off-limits to people without permits. Restaurants that serve alcohol, for example, are open to carry by anyone in possession of a recognized carry permit. But persons without permits may not carry concealed or openly in such areas. Arizona residents have also found that having the permits allows them to more easily secure out-of-state reciprocity.

Persons without recognized permits: Anyone who is law-abiding and at least 21 years old may carry a concealed weapon in his vehicle or on his person in most public areas of the state. He must disclose to law enforcement if asked that he possesses a weapon and should be aware that cities may prohibit any non-permittee from carrying in certain public park areas.

All Persons: Arizona's preemption statute prevents localities from enacting or enforcing most laws regulating the carry, possession or transport of firearms. Gun owners may still be faced with general prohibitions on carry in such obvious areas as schools and polling booths, and some less obvious areas such as "public establishments" (ie. sports arena owned or leased by the government). But, fortunately for the traveler, most property owners are prohibited from enforcing rules that ban firearms in privately-owned vehicles in their parking lots.

Arkansas

Total prohibition   *(+0, improving, but no open carry or unlicensed car carry)*   **Total freedom**

0 ------ 10 ------ 20 ------ 30 ------ 40 ------ 50 ------ 60 ------ 70 ------ 80 ------ 90 ------ 100

Λ

Traveler's checklist:

*Standard firearms ownership: unrestricted, no permit or license required

*Semi-auto / high capacity magazines: no restrictions on possession or sale

*Machine gun ownership: no state restrictions, compliance with federal law only

*Firearm law uniformity: uniform throughout state, local units prohibited from enacting ordinances regulating firearms

*Right of Self-Defense: NRA-model castle doctrine, but *duty to retreat* in public areas

*Open carry: prohibited in public areas under most circumstances

*Concealed carry: licenses granted on a shall issue basis to residents; automatic recognition of carry permits from all other states

*Vehicle carry by non-permittees: handguns must be unloaded and cased; glove compartment carry of a handgun is illegal; rifles and shotguns may be carried in plain view or secured in commercial gun cases

*State Parks: concealed handgun carry by recognized licensees permitted

*Restaurants serving alcohol: permittees may carry while eating in dining areas – p.3

*Duty to notify LEO of permit status: immediately upon contact and request for ID

*Vehicle gun possession at colleges: prohibited if posted, otherwise lawful for permittees

Arkansas's reputation as a rough and ready frontier state in the late 1850s fostered a climate where many a Civil War battle was fought between citizens with opposing sympathies. Privately owned firearms played a key role in determining the outcome of these skirmishes.

Recognized permittees: The State Police issues permits to carry concealed handguns to qualified residents who are U.S. citizens and at least 21 years old. Permits are granted for five-year terms and only allow licensees to carry *concealed* handguns. Arkansas will not grant permits to nonresidents but will recognize carry permits from all other states. Recognized permittees must inform a police officer upon contact that they are carrying a handgun.

A permittee may carry a concealed handgun in his vehicle or on his person in most public areas. But churches (absent consent of church leaders), college buildings (except for some staff), athletic events, parades, bars, state offices (including those in state parks) and restricted areas (per p.6) are off-limits to handgun carry. Most other "prohibited" areas are posted.

Persons without recognized permits: Arkansas prohibits carrying a handgun on or about one's person or in a vehicle if the purpose in carrying the handgun is to employ it as a "weapon." The courts have held that a loaded, readily accessible handgun generally fits the definition of a "weapon." Thus, a non-permittee may not carry a loaded handgun on his person while on foot or in the passenger compartment of his vehicle. Vehicle carry should be limited to a handgun that is unloaded and cased in a trunk or rear storage area.

Arkansas allows those engaged in a "journey" outside their home county to carry a loaded handgun. This exception is narrowly tailored to only apply when the handgun is possessed within your vehicle and you are actually "traveling." Once you reach your destination, the journey is over and the handgun may no longer be in a loaded, readily accessible condition.

All Persons: Shotguns and rifles may be carried in gun racks, gun slings or commercial gun cases but should remain unloaded during hunting season. Open carry of handguns is generally prohibited to everyone, including permittees.

California

0 ------ 10 ------ 20 ------ 30 ------ 40 ------ 50 ------ 60 ------ 70 ------ 80 ------ 90 ------ 100

λ

Traveler's checklist:

*Standard firearms ownership: firearm registration required for all *new* residents

*Semi-auto / high capacity magazines: heavily restricted, all firearms deemed "assault weapons" and magazines over 10 shots may not be brought into the state

*Machine gun ownership: personal machine gun ownership prohibited

*Firearm law uniformity: preemption law, localities may not regulate the licensing or registration of firearms; other areas of regulation may exist

*Right of Self-Defense: no NRA-model castle doctrine

*Open carry: prohibited in any incorporated area; carry in some rural areas is legitimate

*Concealed carry: licenses issued for "good cause" through one's county sheriff; sheriff may impose additional license restrictions; no reciprocity for out-of-state permits

*Vehicle carry by non-permittees: handguns must be unloaded and secured in the trunk or vehicle storage compartment or *locked* in gun cases; rifles and shotguns must be unloaded and should be secured in cases

*State Parks: firearms must be cased, unloaded and kept within a vehicle or campsite

*Restaurants serving alcohol: permittees may carry while eating in dining areas – see p.3

*Duty to notify LEO of permit status: upon demand of police officer

*Vehicle gun possession at colleges: prohibited by law, exception for CA permittees

Changing demographics and a left wing political agenda in Sacramento has made the once Reagan-friendly State of California a nightmare for travelers carrying firearms.

California permittees: The state requires a California-issued license to carry a handgun concealed on your person or loaded and concealed in a vehicle. California does not issue permits to nonresidents and will not recognize out-of-state licenses. Sheriffs may also impose additional carry restrictions on the licenses they issue.

Persons without California permits: Vehicle transport of a handgun is limited to an unloaded handgun *locked* in the trunk or vehicle storage compartment. An unloaded handgun may also be transported in the passenger compartment if it is secured in a *locked* gun case. Handguns may not be kept in the glove compartment or console box. Long guns must be unloaded but need not be in locked containers. "Loaded" is when ammunition is in a firearm's chamber or any attached magazine. Ammunition should be kept in separate containers.

Open carry of loaded firearms on foot is not allowed in most public areas. But loaded handguns carried openly in belt holsters, or long guns employed for sport, are legal in some remote rural areas. Licensed hunters and fishermen may carry loaded firearms while engaged in hunting and fishing. And loaded firearms may also be carried at a campsite or temporary residence such as an "in camp" RV. RVs on public roads would not qualify for this exception.

Open carry of any *unloaded* firearm was recently outlawed in most public areas. Exceptions exist which allow unloaded, open carry in specifically defined areas such as target ranges and shooting clubs. But general carry in public areas is prohibited

All Persons: California's preemption law prohibits localities from regulating most aspects of firearms licensing and registration. But California's prohibitions on the importation of all semi-automatic assault weapons, .50 caliber center-fire rifles and over 10 shot magazines continue to illustrate the cumulative results of decades of state-sanctioned gun control.

Colorado

Total prohibition *(+0, despite Denver, Colorado is still pro-gun)* **Total freedom**

0 ------ 10 ------ 20 ------ 30 ------ 40 ------ 50 ------ 60 ------ 70 ------ 80 ------ 90 ------ 100

Traveler's checklist:

*Standard firearms ownership: unrestricted, no permit or license required

*Semi-auto / high capacity magazines: over 15 shot magazines not lawfully possessed on July 1, 2013 prohibited; semi-auto gun ownership restricted in Denver

*Machine gun ownership: no state restrictions, compliance with federal law only

*Firearm law uniformity: preemption law, localities prohibited from enforcing *most* ordinances regulating firearms ownership and carry

*Right of Self-Defense: NRA castle doctrine, but *stand your ground* in public not codified

*Open carry: unrestricted under state law; localities may regulate this aspect independently

*Concealed carry: licenses granted to residents on a shall issue basis; reciprocity for nonresidents with carry permits from their home states (see p. 65)

*Vehicle carry by non-permittees: firearms may be lawfully carried anywhere in a vehicle; handguns may be loaded, rifles and shotguns must be unloaded

*State Parks: concealed carry of handguns by recognized licensees permitted

*Restaurants serving alcohol: permittees may carry while eating in dining areas – see p.3

*Duty to notify LEO of permit status: upon demand of police officer

*Vehicle gun possession at colleges: lawful for permittees and their handguns only

Colorado still maintains a strong western tradition when it comes to guns. Despite the recent passage of a magazine ban (fueled, in part, by liberal "refugees' from California), the state's gun laws continue to reflect the best of the gun-owning Rocky Mountain West.

Recognized permittees: A license is required to carry a concealed handgun while on foot. The sheriff of a person's home county issues such a permit for a five-year term. Colorado does not issue licenses to nonresidents but will recognize permits issued by states that recognize Colorado permits. Out-of-state permittees must be at least 21 years old and residents of the state that issued the permit for their carry permits to be valid. Permittees are authorized to carry concealed in most public areas except K-12 schools and public buildings with security screenings.

Persons without recognized permits: A loaded handgun may be carried for self-defense anywhere in a vehicle including, but not limited to, the glove compartment, console box or under the seat. Open carry is legitimate everywhere but Denver. The city mandates that all firearms in a vehicle remain concealed from view and any hunting weapons remain unloaded.

While on foot, a person engaged in lawful hunting activities may carry a concealed handgun without a recognized license. Colorado allows open carry in most public areas with three notable exceptions. Cities or counties may prohibit the open carry of handguns in buildings and specific outdoor areas by posting conspicuous signs. Denver limits any personal carry on foot to those who carry concealed with recognized permits. And firearms carry on public transportation is prohibited unless one possesses a recognized license.

All Persons: Long guns may be transported in a vehicle if they are unloaded. "Unloaded" applies only to a weapon's chamber. The magazines may contain live rounds. The only exception is that firearms transported in a snowmobile must also be unloaded in the magazine and secured in gun cases to be legal.

Colorado's magazine ban only affects over 15 shot magazines that were not lawfully owned prior to July 1, 2013. Magazines purchased or possessed before this date are lawful.

Connecticut

Total prohibition *(+0, the bad gets worse as gun makers leave the state in droves)* **Total freedom**

0 ------ 10 ------ 20 ------ 30 ------ 40 ------ 50 ------ 60 ------ 70 ------ 80 ------ 90 ------ 100

Traveler's checklist:

*   ***Standard firearms ownership:** permit or certificate required for all transfers
*   ***Semi-auto / high capacity magazines:** importation of any over 10 shot magazine or any "assault weapon" (anything that looks remotely military) is prohibited
*   ***Machine gun ownership:** heavily restricted, importation into the state prohibited
*   ***Firearm law uniformity:** no preemption statute; local laws may exist in some areas
*   ***Right of Self-Defense:** no NRA-model castle doctrine, *duty to retreat* in public areas
*   ***Open carry:** prohibited in all public areas unless one has a Connecticut permit
*   ***Concealed carry:** temporary permit granted locally allows an individual to obtain a state permit from the state police; out-of-state licensees are afforded *very* limited reciprocity; nonresidents may apply for CT permits
*   ***Vehicle carry by non-permittees:** handgun carry prohibited absent exception; loaded rifles and shotguns prohibited (see below)
*   ***State Parks:** firearms carry prohibited
*   ***Restaurants serving alcohol:** permittees may carry while eating in dining areas – see p.3
*   ***Duty to notify LEO of permit status:** upon demand of police officer
*   ***Vehicle gun possession at colleges:** subject to college administrative policy

Connecticut's gun laws have become more severe over the last twenty years. While residents and nonresidents alike may acquire handgun carry permits through the state police, anyone who lacks a Connecticut permit faces an unfriendly environment for gun carry.

Connecticut permittees: Vehicle carry of any handgun must be accompanied by a Connecticut carry permit. The state police issue these permits after a resident has first obtained a temporary permit from his hometown. A nonresident with a carry permit from his home state may travel to an officially recognized firearms competition or collectors exhibition if he transports his unloaded handgun in a *locked* gun case or in the vehicle's trunk or inaccessible storage area. He should also have proof of the event because Connecticut does not grant *general* recognition of out-of-state carry permits. A pre-registration form or receipt for the event is recommended.

Any U. S. citizen who possesses a carry license issued by another state may apply directly to the state police for a Connecticut permit. Such licenses are valid for five years, cost $70.00 + processing fees and allow concealed and open carry. But given the restrictive nature of Connecticut, open carry by anyone is not advised.

Persons without Connecticut permits: Vehicle carry of a handgun is prohibited without a Connecticut permit. Exceptions exist which allow the transport of unloaded handguns in locked containers from place of purchase to home, etc. But general car carry is prohibited.

Long guns in a vehicle must be unloaded and, in the case of a resident with a grandfathered assault weapon, locked in a case or trunk with a certificate of registration. Recent court decisions have interpreted Connecticut law very strictly with regards to the vehicle transport of firearms. Non-resident travelers should only possess firearms that are securely cased and unloaded per McClure-Volkmer (p. 5) or state statute *29-38d* that mirrors the federal law.

All Persons: Lack of state preemption means that most localities have ordinances prohibiting carry in public parks and government buildings. Also, importation into the state of any "semi-automatic assault weapon" or over 10 shot magazine is prohibited.

Delaware

Total prohibition *(+12, comparative adj., no change, but need for improvement)* **Total freedom**

0 ------ 10 ------ 20 ------ 30 ------ 40 ------ 50 ------ 60 ------ 70 ------ 80 ------ 90 ------ 100

Traveler's checklist:

> ***Standard firearms ownership:*** unrestricted, no permit or license required
> ***Semi-auto / high capacity magazines:*** no restrictions on possession or sale
> ***Machine gun ownership:*** personal ownership of machine guns prohibited
> ***Firearm law uniformity:*** state preemption law, pre-85 laws grandfathered
> ***Right of Self-Defense:*** no NRA-model castle doctrine, *duty to retreat* in public areas
> ***Open carry:*** unrestricted; however, local ordinances prohibiting open carry may exist
> ***Concealed carry:*** licenses granted on a discretionary basis, reciprocity for nonresidents
> with carry permits from certain other states (see p. 65)
> ***Vehicle carry by non-permittees:*** a loaded handgun may be carried openly or
> secured in the trunk; rifles and shotguns must be unloaded while in a vehicle
> ***State Parks:*** possession and carry of firearms prohibited
> ***Restaurants serving alcohol:*** permittees may carry while eating in dining areas – see p.3
> ***Duty to notify LEO of permit status:*** upon demand of police officer
> ***Vehicle gun possession at colleges:*** subject to college administrative policy

Delaware's proximity to northeast liberalism might lead one to suppose that the state's gun laws are as strict as those of New York. Delaware's rural character, however, has helped preserve a laissez-faire view toward firearm ownership uncommon on the East Coast.

Recognized permittees: The state requires a license to carry a concealed firearm. Such permits are issued to residents through the local superior court of each county and allow the concealed, loaded carry of a handgun within a vehicle or on foot in most public areas. Licenses are initially granted for a period of three years and can then be renewed for five years. Delaware does not issue permits to nonresidents but recognizes licenses of nonresidents from states that provide reasonably similar standards for issuance and also recognize Delaware's permits. Permittees may carry firearms in most public areas of the state (see "all persons" below).

Persons without recognized permits: A non-permittee may carry a loaded handgun in his vehicle if the weapon is in plain view (ie. seat or dashboard) or stored in an inaccessible area such as the trunk. Handguns *may not* be carried in the glove compartment or console box or concealed anywhere on or about one's person.

While on foot, a handgun may be carried openly in a visible belt holster. Because carrying a concealed weapon without a license is a felony in Delaware, travelers without permits who carry openly should exercise caution if they intend to possess a firearm while visiting the state. The state preemption law is broad enough to prohibit most new regulation of firearms at the local level. But ordinances predating 1985 are grandfathered by the statute and may still exist in some areas of Delaware's three counties.

All Persons: Shotguns and rifles must be unloaded when transported in any motorized vehicle or watercraft and properly secured in a rear window gun rack or commercial gun case. Long guns must be unloaded regardless of whether a person has a permit. Although Delaware's licensing law technically allows the carry of any firearm by those with recognized permits, long guns are further regulated by conservation laws and must remain unloaded while in a vehicle.

Anyone is prohibited from possessing firearms in state parks/forests, wildlife areas & most universally restricted areas (per p.6). NFA machine gun possession is also prohibited.

District of Columbia

Total prohibition   *(+5, carry law enacted, little practical improvement)*   **Total freedom**

0 ------ 10 ------ 20 ------ 30 ------ 40 ------ 50 ------ 60 ------ 70 ------ 80 ------ 90 ------ 100

人

Traveler's checklist:

   Standard firearms ownership: restricted, handguns, rifles and shotguns must be
           registered and stored in a disassembled state until the weapons need to be used

   Semi-auto / high capacity magazines: totally restricted; ownership of any military-
           pattern weapon or over 10-shot magazine prohibited

   Machine gun ownership: totally restricted; ownership of any Class III item
           (machine gun, suppressor or short-barreled rifle) prohibited

   Firearm law uniformity: laws are uniformly strict throughout the district

   Right of Self-Defense: no NRA-model castle doctrine

   Open carry: prohibited anywhere in the District

   Concealed carry: licenses issued to residents and non-residents on a discretionary basis
           through the chief of police; no reciprocity for out-of-state carry permits

   Vehicle carry by non-permittees: firearms must be unloaded, cased and locked in the
           trunk, vehicles without trunks may substitute a locked container within
           the vehicle other than the glove compartment (see below)

   State Parks: n/a

   Restaurants serving alcohol: all firearms carry prohibited

   Duty to notify LEO of permit status: immediately upon official contact

   Vehicle gun possession at colleges: prohibited by law

In 2014, D.C. city council enacted emergency legislation providing for the issuance of concealed carry licenses to qualified persons. The resulting law is highly restrictive and practically ineffective for most gun owners hoping to carry for self-defense outside their homes.

Washington D.C. permittees: A license is required to carry a concealed pistol on one's person or in a vehicle. Such permits are issued by the Chief of Police to qualified persons who are at least 21 years old for 2 year terms. The applicant must demonstrate a specific personal need to be issued a license. The District will not recognize carry permits issued by other states but will issue permits to residents and non-residents. Licensees may only carry *concealed* handguns and are prohibited from carry in most public areas including government buildings, schools (including colleges), child care facilities, hospitals, public transportation (including Metrorail), public gatherings & demonstrations, bars & restaurants serving alcohol, stadiums, public memorials, and all private residences (absent owner consent). Any licensee approaching these prohibited areas must immediately unload his handgun and secure it in his locked vehicle. Permittees must also declare their permit status upon any official contact with law enforcement.

Non-Residents without D.C. permits: Those without D.C. permits are prohibited from carrying any firearms or ammunition in the District. Such items may be transported *through* the District if the firearms are unloaded, cased and locked in the trunk or, in a vehicle without a trunk, secured in a locked container (other than a glove compartment or console box). Any ammunition must be separate from the guns. The traveler may not stop anywhere in the District or his "passing through" status will cease to exist and his firearms would be subject to seizure.

Recent reports indicate that persons have been arrested for having one spent ammunition cartridge in the passenger compartment of their vehicle. Anyone traveling *through* the District should exercise extreme caution when transporting firearms or ammunition.

Florida

Total prohibition   *(+2, remains pro-gun despite shifting demographics)*   Total freedom

0 ------ 10 ------ 20 ------ 30 ------ 40 ------ 50 ------ 60 ------ 70 ------ 80 ------ 90 ------ 100

Traveler's checklist:

    ***Standard firearms ownership:** unrestricted, no permit or license required

    ***Semi-auto / high capacity magazines:** no restrictions on possession or sale

    ***Machine gun ownership:** no state restrictions, compliance with federal law only

    ***Firearm law uniformity:** state preemption law, gun laws uniform throughout state

    ***Right of Self-Defense:** NRA-model castle doctrine, *stand your ground* in public areas

    ***Open carry:** prohibited in all public areas

    ***Concealed carry:** license granted on a "shall issue" basis; reciprocity available for nonresidents with carry permits from their home states (see p. 65)

    ***Vehicle carry by non-permittees:** firearms may be concealed and loaded while carried in a private vehicle provided they are "securely encased or otherwise not readily accessible" (see below)

    ***State Parks:** concealed handgun carry by recognized licensees permitted

    ***Restaurants serving alcohol:** permittees may carry while eating in dining areas – see p.3

    ***Duty to notify LEO of permit status:** upon demand of police officer

    ***Vehicle gun possession at colleges:** lawful for gun owners at all public universities

Florida's status as a popular vacation destination results in quite a few visitors to the state every year. These people will be pleased to know that Florida's firearms laws are generally favorable for the occasional traveler so long as several important aspects are kept in mind.

Recognized permittees: A license is required to carry a concealed firearm on foot or in a vehicle. The Division of Licensing issues such permits to qualified persons 21 years and older for a seven-year term. These permits allow the carry of handguns, knives and stun guns.

Florida issues licenses to nonresidents and recognizes permits from states whose laws provide for recognition of Florida permits. Out-of-state permittees must have immediate possession of their permits, reside in the state where the permit was issued and be at least 21 years of age. Florida prohibits carry in most universally restricted areas (see p. 6) as well as scholastic and professional athletic events not related to firearms, college campuses, career centers, mental health facilities and places of nuisance (illegal gambling and prostitution houses).

Persons without recognized permits: Carry in a private vehicle is allowed if the firearm is *securely encased* or is *not otherwise readily accessible*. *Securely encased* includes carry in a snapped holster (off one's person), glove compartment, gun case or a closed box or container. *Not readily accessible* means locked in the trunk of a car or the storage compartment of a pick-up truck or RV. Either of these conditions is legal for non-licensed carry. Carry in a public vehicle, such as a bus, is allowed when the firearm is securely encased and not in the person's manual possession. But firearms concealed *on the person* while occupying any vehicle are illegal. This would include a gun under one's clothing or hidden anywhere on the person.

All Persons: Open carry while on foot is not permitted in any public area. This prohibition includes licensees and non-licensees. The state also prohibits most businesses from preventing customers or employees from possessing firearms in their locked vehicles while those vehicles are parked on company grounds. Florida's preemption law prevents localities from regulating most aspects of firearm ownership and provides penalties for any locality's willful infringement. With the exception of some zoning laws, firearm regulation is uniform in the state.

Georgia

Total prohibition   *(+5, carry options expanded and preemption strengthened)*   **Total freedom**

0 ------ 10 ------ 20 ------ 30 ------ 40 ------ 50 ------ 60 ------ 70 ------ 80 ------ 90 ------ 100

Traveler's checklist:

  *Standard firearms ownership: unrestricted, no permit or license required
  *Semi-auto / high capacity magazines: no restrictions on possession or sale
  *Machine gun ownership: compliance with relevant portions of federal law only
  *Firearm law uniformity: preemption law, firearm laws uniform throughout state
  *Right of Self-Defense: NRA-model castle doctrine, *stand your ground* in public areas
  *Open carry: prohibited unless one possesses a recognized license (see exceptions below)
  *Concealed carry: licenses granted to residents on a "shall issue" basis; reciprocity
      available for non-residents from certain other states (see p. 65)
  *Vehicle carry by non-permittees: loaded firearms may be transported anywhere
      in a private passenger vehicle (see below for details)
  *State Parks: concealed handgun carry by recognized licensees permitted
  *Restaurants serving alcohol: permittees may carry while eating in dining areas – see p.3
  *Duty to notify LEO of permit status: upon demand of police officer
  *Vehicle gun possession at colleges: lawful for permittees

Despite the growth of urban areas such as Atlanta, Georgia maintains a distinctly rural character when it comes to gun regulation. Some cities, such as Kennesaw, even require all citizens to possess at least one firearm in their home for self-defense.

Recognized permittees: The state requires a license to carry a weapon (handgun or knife) on one's person in a concealed or open manner. Georgia issues permits through the probate court of an applicant's home county to qualified persons 21 years or older for five year terms. The state does not issue permits to nonresidents but recognizes permits from states that also recognize Georgia permits as long as the permittee is not a resident of Georgia. Military persons are exempt from needing a license and may use their military IDs as proof of this exemption. Recognized permittees may carry in most public areas except churches (unless allowed by church), school safety zones (K-12 & colleges), courthouses, mental health facilities, businesses that post signs and state & local government buildings with security screenings. Parking facilities in most prohibited areas are legitimate if the licensee keeps the firearm locked in his vehicle.

Persons without recognized permits: A non-permittee who is not prohibited by law from possessing a handgun may carry a loaded firearm anywhere in his *own* vehicle, home or place of business. Someone who qualifies for, but does not possess, a Georgia weapons license (ie. 21 years or older and *not* a felon, illegal drug user or patient at a mental hospital or drug treatment center) may carry a loaded firearm in any vehicle he occupies. While a non-permittee is on foot, he may carry a handgun provided the weapon is unloaded and cased.

Open carry of a loaded handgun is prohibited in most public areas without a recognized license. But hunters and sportsmen may carry loaded handguns on their persons while hunting, fishing or shooting so long as they possesses the necessary state permits for those activities (if such permits are required) and have the permission of the owner upon whose land they operate.

All Persons: Any person who is not prohibited from possessing a firearm may carry a loaded long gun while on foot in most public areas without a permit as long as the gun remains in the "open and fully exposed" to view. Because carry permits only authorize handgun or knife carry, licensees & non-licensees would be required to carry their loaded long guns in this manner.

Hawaii

Total prohibition *(+0, Aloha state is the "good-bye" state for gun owners)* **Total freedom**

0 ------ 10 ------ 20 ------ 30 ------ 40 ------ 50 ------ 60 ------ 70 ------ 80 ------ 90 ------ 100

Traveler's checklist:

*Standard firearms ownership: restricted, registration required within 72 hrs of arrival

*Semi-auto / high capacity magazines: pistol magazines over 10 shots prohibited; ownership or possession of "assault pistols" prohibited

*Machine gun ownership: individual ownership of machine guns prohibited

*Firearm law uniformity: no preemption law, localities may pass their own gun laws

*Right of Self-Defense: no NRA-model castle doctrine, *duty to retreat* in public areas

*Open carry: prohibited in all public areas

*Concealed carry: license issued on a discretionary basis, valid only in county where issued; no reciprocity for carry permits from other states

*Vehicle carry by non-permittees: firearms generally not allowed in vehicles unless one has a Hawaii permit to carry. (see below for exceptions)

*State Parks: firearms must remain cased, unloaded and stowed in a vehicle

*Restaurants serving alcohol: permittees may carry while eating in dining areas – see p.3

*Duty to notify LEO of permit status: upon demand of police officer

*Vehicle gun possession at colleges: subject to college administrative policy

Although it is doubtful anyone would ever take a "road trip" to Hawaii (absent construction of a very long bridge), travelers to America's fiftieth state may still find themselves inquiring about state regulation involving the carry and possession of firearms. Hawaii has very strict laws in this area making firearm ownership, especially by non-residents, next to impossible.

Hawaii permittees: Hawaii requires a permit to carry a loaded, concealed handgun on one's person or in a vehicle. Residents and non-residents who are at least 21 years old, U.S. citizens or official representatives of foreign governments may apply to any chief of police for a permit that is valid in that county for a one year term and allows the concealed carry of a handgun only. Hawaii does not recognize permits from other states and operates as a "may issue" domain. Consequently, very few permits have been issued to citizens in the last thirty years.

Persons without Hawaii permits: Vehicular travel is extremely limited for all firearms. It is unlawful to carry rifles, shotguns or handguns in a vehicle unless one has a permit. An exception to this general prohibition allows a person to transport unloaded and securely cased firearms from the point of purchase to home or from home to a firing range, police station, place of formal hunter or shooter education or repair shop. Non-residents may have a difficult time fitting into one of these exceptions unless they have relatives living in Hawaii. Concealed or open carry of a firearm by anyone on foot is strictly prohibited unless one is engaged in lawful hunting with a proper permit. A hunter may then carry an unconcealed, loaded pistol as long as that pistol and its ammunition have been approved for hunting in accordance with state statutes.

All Persons: All firearms must be registered with authorities within seventy-two hours of entering the state. Handguns may not be possessed without first acquiring an approval permit from the police. Shotguns and rifles do not require a possession permit. But registration is still mandatory. Personal ownership of machine guns or any other Class III items is strictly prohibited. Semi-automatic military rifles are currently treated the same as rifles and shotguns with increased regulation a possibility. Assault pistols such as the TEC-9 and M-11 are prohibited along with any high capacity pistol magazine capable of holding more than ten rounds.

Idaho

Total prohibition *(+2, pioneer spirit & lots of guns make Idaho the place to live)* **Total freedom**

| 0 ------ 10 ------ 20 ------ 30 ------ 40 ------ 50 ------ 60 ------ 70 ------ 80 ------ 90 ------ 100 |

Traveler's checklist:

- ***Standard firearms ownership:** unrestricted, no permit or license required
- ***Semi-auto / high capacity magazines:** no restrictions on possession or sale
- ***Machine gun ownership:** no state restrictions, compliance with federal law only
- ***Firearm law uniformity:** preemption law, firearm laws uniform throughout state
- ***Right of Self-Defense:** NRA castle doctrine, but *stand your ground* in public not codified
- ***Open carry:** unrestricted in most public areas and generally accepted
- ***Concealed carry:** licenses issued on a "shall issue" basis; automatic recognition of carry permits from all other states
- ***Vehicle carry by non-permittees:** loaded handguns may be carried in plain view; loaded rifles and shotguns may be in plain view or cased
- ***State Parks:** concealed handgun carry by recognized licensees permitted
- ***Restaurants serving alcohol:** permittees may carry while eating in dining areas – see p.3
- ***Duty to notify LEO of permit status:** upon demand of police officer
- ***Vehicle gun possession at colleges:** lawful for ID enhanced permittees & retired LEOs

Idaho's frontier heritage provides the traveler with a gun-friendly environment while cruising the state's northern panhandle. In Idaho, firearms are much like potatoes. Both are considered essential to defining the state's classic character.

Recognized permittees: A license is required to carry a handgun concealed on or about one's person while on foot or in a vehicle. Permits (both regular & enhanced) are issued by any county sheriff to qualified persons 21 years or older for a 5 year term. Idaho will issue permits to nonresidents as well as recognize any permit issued by another state or locality. The attorney general may execute agreements with other states for the recognition of Idaho permits in those states. A recognized permittee may carry a concealed handgun in most public areas. Idaho prohibits carry in only the most obvious places such as jails, courthouses and schools.

Persons without recognized permits: Travelers without permits may carry loaded handguns in their vehicles if the weapons are in plain view. For a handgun to be in plain view, it must be discernible to ordinary observation and not hidden either on one's person or in close proximity thereof. A holstered handgun on the vehicle's dash or passenger seat is acceptable. Under the seat would be considered concealed and thus illegal. Inside the glove compartment or console box is acceptable if the handgun is unloaded. Unloaded or disassembled handguns are exempt from statutes regulating concealed carry and may be transported anywhere in the vehicle.

Open carry of a firearm while on foot is legitimate as long the weapon is visible to casual observation. Concealed carry is also allowed under certain circumstances to non-permittees. Outside any incorporated town or city, handguns may be concealed so long as the concealment does not occur within a vehicle or on a public highway. This allowance generally applies to outdoor recreational activities where firearms carry is quite common.

All Persons: Idaho's prohibition on carrying concealed weapons does not apply to lawfully possessed rifles and shotguns. These firearms may be carried loaded and exposed to view or secured in commercial gun cases anywhere in the vehicle. Idaho's strengthened preemption law prevents any local regulation of firearms and ensures the right of enhanced permittees and retired LEOs to possess firearms in outdoor areas on state university campuses.

Illinois

Total prohibition   *(-12, carry law euphoria tempered by numerous restrictions)*   **Total freedom**

0 ------ 10 ------ 20 ------ 30 ------ 40 ------ 50 ------ 60 ------ 70 ------ 80 ------ 90 ------ 100

Traveler's checklist:

* **Standard firearms ownership:** restricted, firearm identification card required
* **Semi-auto gun / high capacity magazines:** firearm identification card required; local restrictions on assault rifles and high capacity magazines possible
* **Machine gun ownership:** personal machine gun ownership prohibited
* **Firearm law uniformity:** preemption law, handgun regulation preempted; ordinances regulating long guns, "assault rifles" & laser sights still exist
* **Right of Self-Defense:** no NRA castle doctrine, *stand your ground* in public not codified
* **Open carry:** prohibited in all public areas
* **Concealed carry:** licenses issued to qualified residents and nonresidents on a "shall issue" basis; no reciprocity for out-of-state permits
* **Vehicle carry by non-residents:** any nonresident who has a carry permit issued by his home state may carry a loaded handgun in his vehicle; long guns must remain unloaded and cased if the possessor has a carry permit or a FOID card; if the nonresident lacks a permit, he must also stow any firearms in the trunk
* **State Parks:** concealed handgun carry by Illinois licensees permitted in most outdoor areas
* **Restaurant serving alcohol:** permittees may carry while eating in dining areas – p.3
* **Duty to notify LEO of permit status:** upon demand of police officer
* **Vehicle gun possession at colleges:** lawful for permittees; but subject to college policy

Illinois finally joined the ranks of the nation's 49 other states by enacting a concealed carry law. The law and accompanying preemption statute are marked improvements over what had been a "no public carry" norm in the "Land of Lincoln."

Illinois permittees: A license is required to carry a loaded handgun concealed on or about ones person in public or in a vehicle. The Illinois State Police will issue such a license for a 5-year term to a qualified person who is 21 years or older. Illinois does not recognize out-of-state permits, but will issue permits to nonresidents from approved states for a $300.00 fee.

An Illinois permittee is quite limited as to where he can legally carry. Prohibited areas include childcare facilities, govt. buildings, courts, schools, hospitals, nursing homes, buses & trains, bars, permitted public gatherings, special events serving alcohol, playgrounds, local parks (except trails), colleges, casinos, stadiums, amusement parks, airports, libraries, museums, zoos and private property owners who choose to prohibit carry. All these areas must post signs alerting visitors to the prohibitions. And permittees are allowed to keep their concealed handguns in the trunk or glove compartment of their vehicles while in the parking lots of these areas.

Non-residents: A non-resident who can legally carry a firearm in public in his home state may carry a concealed, loaded handgun in his vehicle. This exception only applies to nonresidents and is practically limited to those with carry permits from their home states. If the non-resident leaves his vehicle unattended, all firearms should be stored in locked containers.

All Persons: Long guns in a vehicle must remain cased and unloaded regardless of permit status. If a nonresident lacks a valid permit, he must also stow these weapons in the trunk. Illinois prohibits open carry and allows some localities to ban assault weapon possession. And even though all regulation of handgun-related issues is preempted by the state, some cities, such as Chicago, are still enforcing ordinances prohibiting laser sights.

Indiana

Total prohibition *(+4, great for permittees, still tough for those w/o permits)* **Total freedom**

0 ------ 10 ------ 20 ------ 30 ------ 40 ------ 50 ------ 60 ------ 70 ------ 80 ------ 90 ------ 100

Traveler's checklist:

*Standard firearms ownership: unrestricted, no permit or license required

*Semi-auto / high capacity magazines: no restrictions on possession or sale

*Machine gun ownership: compliance with relevant provisions of federal law

*Firearm law uniformity: preemption law, firearm laws uniform throughout state

*Right of Self-Defense: NRA-model castle doctrine, *stand your ground* in public areas

*Open carry: prohibited unless one possesses a recognized permit

*Concealed carry: licenses granted on a "shall issue" basis; automatic recognition for non-residents with carry permits from other states

*Vehicle carry by non-permittees: handguns must be unloaded, cased and stowed in the trunk or rear storage area; loaded rifles and shotguns may be carried in the passenger compartment but should be secured in cases

*State Parks: concealed handgun carry by recognized licensees permitted

*Restaurants serving alcohol: permittees may carry while eating in dining areas – see p.3

*Duty to notify LEO of permit status: upon demand of police officer

*Vehicle gun possession at colleges: subject to college administrative policy

Indiana has one of America's oldest "shall issue" carry laws. Since 1935, Indiana has allowed residents and nonresidents with regular places of employment or business in the state to obtain licenses to carry loaded handguns for personal protection.

Recognized permittees: Indiana issues licenses that are valid for four years, cost less than $50.00 and allow both concealed and open carry. Residents, and non-residents who work in Indiana, are eligible. Residents may also apply for more expensive lifetime carry licenses. Such permits are valid for the applicant's life. Nonresidents with out-of-state permits are granted automatic recognition for handgun carry but must comply with whatever restrictions exist on their out-of- state permits. For example, if the permit requires the handgun to remain concealed, then it must remain concealed even though Indiana law allows open carry with a permit.

Recognized permittees may carry their loaded handguns in most public areas. Some notable exceptions for the traveler would be riverboats, K-12 schools and the state fair. These areas are off-limits to any licensee unless he leaves his firearm locked in his vehicle.

Indiana's preemption law makes local regulation of licensees virtually non-existent. Localities may still prohibit carry in courthouses, hospitals and some special events. But attempting regulation anywhere else could result in stiff legal sanctions against the locality.

Persons without recognized permits: Vehicle carry of a handgun is prohibited unless the weapon is securely cased and unloaded in a manner that renders it not readily accessible for immediate use. Stowage in the trunk or rear most portion of an SUV or RV would satisfy this requirement. Open or concealed carry of loaded handguns by unlicensed persons is generally not allowed in Indiana unless the individual is engaged in legal hunting activity, shooting at a target range or attending a firearms instructional course.

All Persons: Vehicle carry of loaded long guns is allowed in most places except property owned by Indiana's Dept. of Nat'l Resources. Courts have held that pistol grip shotguns with no shoulder stocks are classified as handguns and require a carry permit. Also, employees of most businesses may keep firearms in their vehicles while parked on company property.

Iowa

Total prohibition   *(+0, improving for permittees, still tough for non-permittees)*   **Total freedom**

0 ------ 10 ------ 20 ------ 30 ------ 40 ------ 50 ------ 60 ------ 70 ------ 80 ------ 90 ------ 100

Traveler's checklist:

* ***Standard firearms ownership:** no license required (except for handgun purchase)
* ***Semi-auto / high capacity magazines:** no restrictions on possession or sale
* ***Machine gun ownership:** private ownership of machine guns prohibited
* ***Firearm law uniformity:** preemption law, firearm laws uniform throughout state
* ***Right of Self-Defense:** no NRA-model castle doctrine, *duty to retreat* in public areas
* ***Open carry:** generally prohibited unless one possesses a recognized permit to carry
* ***Concealed carry:** licenses issued on a "shall issue" basis; automatic recognition for non-residents with carry permits from other states; Iowa will issue "professional" permits to non-residents
* ***Vehicle carry by non-permittees:** handguns may not be carried in a loaded or accessible condition; rifles and shotguns must be unloaded and cased yet may be accessible to passengers
* ***State Parks:** concealed handgun carry by recognized licensees permitted
* ***Restaurants serving alcohol:** permittees may carry while eating in dining areas – see p.3
* ***Duty to notify LEO of permit status:** upon demand of police officer
* ***Vehicle gun possession at colleges:** prohibited by law

Iowa recently joined the majority of states with "shall issue" concealed carry. And while the state's treatment of firearms may be stricter than other "bread basket" states of the Midwest, handgun carry for recognized permittees has become much easier.

Recognized permittees: Iowa requires a license to carry a loaded firearm (handgun or long gun) in a vehicle or on one's person while on foot. The state issues professional & non-professional licenses. Non-professional licenses are granted through the sheriff of one's home county to any qualified resident who is at least 21 years old. The licenses are valid for five years and allow open or concealed carry of any firearm in most public areas. Notable exceptions would include casinos, the state fair, the state capitol, universities and carry on ATVs and snowmobiles.

Professional licenses are granted to residents through their local sheriff and to non-residents through the Department of Public Safety. The professional licenses are available to anyone 18 years or older whose need to go armed arises out of their employment. Iowa recognizes any valid, out-of-state carry permit so long as the permittee is not a resident of Iowa.

Persons without recognized permits: A non-permittee may only transport handguns in a vehicle which are unloaded and contained inside a closed or fastened container which is too large to conceal on one's person. Handguns may also be transported in a cargo or luggage area where the weapons are inaccessible to the vehicle's occupants. Long guns may remain accessible to passengers if the weapons are unloaded and cased.

Handguns may not be carried on one's person, either concealed or openly, within any municipal limits without a recognized permit. An exception exists which allows persons on recognized target ranges or hunting preserves to carry openly as long as they have the permission of the owner. But public carry of a loaded handgun is generally not allowed without a permit.

All Persons: Iowa prohibits the possession of machine guns, short-barreled rifles and shotguns. The only exception would be for historical reenactors who use firearms classified as "curios and relics."   The weapons must also be rendered inoperable before entering the state.

Kansas

Λ

Traveler's checklist:

- ***Standard firearms ownership:** unrestricted, no permit or license required
- ***Semi-auto / high capacity magazines:** no restrictions on possession or sale
- ***Machine gun ownership:** compliance with relevant portions of federal law only
- ***Firearm law uniformity:** preemption law, firearm laws uniform throughout state
- ***Right of Self-Defense:** NRA-model castle doctrine, *stand your ground* in public areas
- ***Open carry:** unrestricted under state law; localities may still prohibit carry in certain bldgs.
- ***Concealed carry:** licenses issued to residents on a "shall issue" basis; automatic recognition for non-residents with carry permits from other states
- ***Vehicle carry by non-permittees:** loaded firearms may be carried in plain view or kept in glove compartment or other container (may not be concealed *on one's person*)
- ***State Parks:** concealed handgun carry by recognized licensees permitted
- ***Restaurants serving alcohol:** permittees may carry if premises are not "posted" – see p.3
- ***Duty to notify LEO of permit status:** upon demand of police officer
- ***Vehicle gun possession at colleges:** lawful for permittees

Kansas' tradition of private gun ownership was exemplified in 1892 when citizens of Coffeyville used their personal firearms to defeat the Dalton gang's attempt to rob the town's two banks. This historical connection to a vibrant gun culture is perhaps why the people of Kansas overwhelmingly voted to add a "right to bear arms" clause to their constitution in 2010.

Recognized permittees: The attorney general will issue a license to carry a concealed handgun through the sheriff of the applicant's home county for a four-year term. Such permits are only available to residents who are U.S. citizens and at least 21 years old. Kansas will recognize any valid, out-of-state permit so long as the permittee is not a resident of Kansas. A recognized permittee may carry a concealed handgun in most public areas. Prohibited places can include most any private or public building that chooses to restrict carry. But the building *must* be posted with A.G. approved signage for the prohibition to be enforceable. Only the buildings, and not the parking lots, of these areas are off-limits to carry.

Persons without recognized permits: A non-permittee may carry a loaded handgun in his vehicle if the weapon is not "*concealed on the person*" (ie. under one's clothing or garment). Plain view (dashboard or front seat), glove compartment, console box or trunk would be legitimate areas for stowage. Kansas recently amended its preemption law to eliminate any local ordinances regulating vehicle transportation of loaded firearms by non-permittees.

Open carry of a handgun while on foot and concealed carry by sportsmen engaged in hunting and fishing are also allowed. Most local ordinances regulating these areas have been eliminated by recent amendments to the state's preemption law. But building owners (both private and municipal) may still prohibit open carry within their locations.

All Persons: Kansas' concealed carry law only licenses the carry of handguns or other weapons designed to be fired "by the use of a single hand." Rifles and shotguns are not covered. So no one may carry a loaded long gun *concealed on his person*. But open carry of loaded long guns is lawful in most public areas except posted property, school zones and federal facilities.

Tribal lands (casinos, etc.) generally recognize licensees but may not be as likely to extend the same courtesies to non-licensees. Rules in these areas may vary by reservation.

Kentucky

Total prohibition *(-2, residents w/ out-of-state permits no longer recognized)* **Total freedom**

0 ------ 10 ------ 20 ------ 30 ------ 40 ------ 50 ------ 60 ------ 70 ------ 80 ------ 90 ------ 100

Traveler's checklist:

*   ***Standard firearms ownership:** unrestricted, no permit or license required
*   ***Semi-auto / high capacity magazines:** no restrictions on possession or sale
*   ***Machine gun ownership:** no state restrictions, compliance with federal law only
*   ***Firearm law uniformity:** preemption law, firearm laws uniform throughout state
*   ***Right of Self-Defense:** NRA-model castle doctrine, *stand your ground* in public areas
*   ***Open carry:** unrestricted in most public areas and generally accepted
*   ***Concealed carry:** licenses granted to residents on a "shall issue" basis; automatic recognition for non-residents with carry permits from other states
*   ***Vehicle carry by non-permittees:** loaded firearms may be carried in plain view or stowed in any factory-installed vehicle compartment
*   ***State Parks:** concealed handgun carry by recognized licensees permitted
*   ***Restaurants serving alcohol:** permittees may carry while eating in dining areas – see p.3
*   ***Duty to notify LEO of permit status:** upon demand of police officer
*   ***Vehicle gun possession at colleges:** lawful for any gun owner

Kentucky's rolling hills and tree-covered mountains provide the perfect setting for a movie about the early pioneers of the Ohio valley. Firearms carry in those days was essential for survival. And Kentucky still maintains a healthy respect for this heritage in its firearm laws.

Recognized permittees: Kentucky requires a license to carry a firearm, or any other deadly weapon, concealed on or about one's person. The State Police issue permits through the sheriff of the applicant's home county for a five-year term. Kentucky does not grant permits to nonresidents but will recognize any permit issued by another state as long as the permittee is not a resident of Kentucky. A recognized permittee may carry concealed in most public areas. Prohibited places include childcare centers, bars, legislative meetings, law enforcement offices and courthouses. Colleges, hospitals, local governments, and private businesses may also ban carry in their buildings by posting signs. But prohibitions in these areas are not criminal offenses.

Persons without recognized permits: Loaded firearms may be carried in a vehicle if the weapons are in plain view. A loaded handgun can be in a visible belt holster or on the dashboard or passenger seat of one's car. Loaded long guns may be secured in gun racks or commercial gun cases anywhere in the vehicle except concealed about the person.

Kentucky also allows weapons to be hidden from view in any factory-installed vehicle compartment, whether locked or unlocked. Console boxes, seat pockets, glove compartments or trunks are among the acceptable areas for unlicensed concealment.

Any landowner, sole proprietor or lessee may carry concealed without a permit on property they own or rent. Also, anyone with the permission of the property owner may carry.

A traveler may openly carry a loaded handgun while on foot in most public areas. Such carry is best limited to visible belt holsters secured on one's hip. Kentucky's strong preemption law now provides stiff penalties for any locality that attempts to regulate this activity.

All Persons: A property owner may not prohibit employees and customers from carrying firearms in their vehicles while the vehicles are parked on that owner's property. Civil penalties exist for property owners that act contrary to this mandate. Also, game wardens may not harass any sportsmen who carry firearms for self-defense while hunting or fishing.

Louisiana

Total prohibition *(+3, restaurant carry O.K., things just gets better in the bayou)* Total freedom

0 ------ 10 ------ 20 ------ 30 ------ 40 ------ 50 ------ 60 ------ 70 ------ 80 ------ 90 ------ 100

Traveler's checklist:

*   ***Standard firearms ownership:** unrestricted, no permit or license required
*   ***Semi-auto / high capacity magazines:** no restrictions on possession or sale
*   ***Machine gun ownership:** ownership restricted to "war relic" machine guns
*   ***Firearm law uniformity:** preemption law, localities prohibited from enacting any ordinances after 1985 that regulate firearms (some exceptions, see below)
*   ***Right of Self-Defense:** NRA-model castle doctrine, *stand your ground* in public areas
*   ***Open carry:** unrestricted in most public areas and generally accepted
*   ***Concealed carry:** licenses granted on a "shall issue" basis; reciprocity available for non-residents with carry permits from certain other states (see p. 65)
*   ***Vehicle carry by non-permittees:** loaded firearms may be carried openly or in the glove compartment, console box, or trunk of vehicle
*   ***State Parks:** concealed handgun carry by recognized licensees permitted
*   ***Restaurant serving alcohol:** permittees may carry while eating in dining areas – see p.3
*   ***Duty to notify LEO of permit status:** immediately upon official contact
*   ***Vehicle gun possession at colleges:** lawful for any gun owner

Louisiana is called "The Sportsman's Paradise" for its vast network of game preserves. This condition, along with the state's political conservatism, ensures a strong respect for firearms that most gun-owning travelers will find very refreshing.

Recognized permittees: Louisiana requires a license to carry a handgun concealed upon one's person. Such permits are issued by the Department of Public Safety to qualified residents who are 21 or older for five years or a lifetime, depending upon the choice of the applicant. Louisiana does not grant permits to nonresidents but will recognize licenses issued by states whose laws also recognize Louisiana permits. Recognized permittees must be at least 21 years old and may not be Louisiana residents. Permittees may carry in most public areas except churches, parades, the state capitol, bars, and many parts of college campuses. Permittees must also declare their identity to police when approached by an officer.

Persons without recognized permits: A loaded handgun may be carried almost anywhere in a vehicle. The glove compartment, console box, seat pocket or dashboard are all legitimate placement areas. Plain view carry in a snapped holster or other similar carry rig is also acceptable as long as one's clothing does not cover the handgun.

Loaded rifles and shotguns may be carried in commercial gun cases, gun racks or outside storage compartments. The state only restricts weapons that are concealed *on one's person*. This prohibition would include firearms hidden under one's shirt, jacket or outer garment as well as weapons contained within any purse or briefcase carried by a person.

A handgun may be carried openly while on foot in most public areas. The weapon should be exposed to view in a snapped belt holster. Open carry is common throughout the state.

All Persons: Louisiana's preemption law prevents localities from regulating most facets of firearm possession. But ordinances enacted before July, 1985 are grandfathered. And some local restrictions on carry in public buildings and commercial establishments are possible. Vehicle carry on most public and private parking lots is protected activity that is shielded by state law from any outright prohibitions by the property owners.

Maine

Total prohibition (*+0, good, but needs improvement for vehicle carry w/o permit*) **Total freedom**

0 ------ 10 ------ 20 ------ 30 ------ 40 ------ 50 ------ 60 ------ 70 ------ 80 ------ 90 ------ 100

Traveler's checklist:

- ***Standard firearms ownership:*** unrestricted, no permit or license required
- ***Semi-auto gun / high capacity magazines:*** no restrictions on possession or sale
- ***Machine gun ownership:*** no state restrictions, compliance with federal law only
- ***Firearm law uniformity:*** preemption law, firearm laws uniform throughout state
- ***Open carry:*** unrestricted under state law in most public areas
- ***Right of Self-Defense:*** no NRA-model castle doctrine, *duty to retreat* in public areas
- ***Concealed carry:*** license granted on a "shall issue" basis; reciprocity available for nonresidents with carry permits from their home states (see p.65)
- ***Vehicle carry by non-permittees:*** firearms must be unloaded and may be carried in plain view, secured in a case or stowed in the trunk or storage compartment
- ***State Parks:*** concealed handgun carry by recognized licensees permitted (except Baxter S.P.)
- ***Restaurants serving alcohol:*** permittees may carry if premises are not "posted" – see p.3
- ***Duty to notify LEO of permit status:*** upon demand of police officer
- ***Vehicle gun possession at colleges:*** subject to college administrative policy

Maine is well known for its "back country" reputation. The state will provide some beautiful scenery as well as a friendly atmosphere for gun owners. But travelers should be aware of several aspects of Maine's law that make it different from states with similar demographics.

Recognized permittees: Maine requires a license to carry a loaded handgun in a vehicle or concealed on or about one's person. The mayor or police chief of a resident's hometown issues such permits to qualified persons 18 years or older for a four year term. A nonresident may apply for a permit by contacting the State Police. Maine will recognize licenses from states that meet or exceed Maine's issuance standards. The out-of-state permittee must also be a resident of the state issuing the permit. Recognized permittees may carry concealed, loaded handguns throughout the state. But travelers should note that casinos, restaurants serving alcohol that post against carry and most of the state capitol are off-limits to all firearms carry.

Persons without recognized permits: A non-permittee may carry a handgun in his vehicle if the weapon is unloaded and in plain view. Any loaded weapon, as well as any handgun carried in the glove compartment, console box or under one's seat, is illegal. Unloaded handguns that are securely encased may be transported in the passenger compartment, trunk or rear storage area as long as the weapons are not readily accessible. Magazines may be loaded but may not be attached to, or inserted in, any firearm.

While on foot, a non-permittee may openly carry a loaded handgun. But travelers should be aware that Maine prohibits the "threatening display" of any firearm. Persons should exercise caution when exposing a handgun and keep the weapon in a snapped holster at all times.

A licensed hunter or trapper may carry a concealed firearm without a recognized permit if he is on foot and actually engaged in hunting or trapping. The state's preemption law prevents any local regulation of this and other firearm rights.

All Persons: Maine's hunting laws forbid the carry of any *loaded* firearms in a vehicle. But a specific exemption allows persons with valid concealed carry permits to possess loaded handguns. Rifles and shotguns are not included in this exemption. So even a recognized permittee should keep his long guns unloaded and cased while occupying a vehicle.

Maryland

Total prohibition   *(+0, Baltimore politics make it a nightmare for gun owners)*   **Total freedom**

0 ------ 10 ------ 20 ------ 30 ------ 40 ------ 50 ------ 60 ------ 70 ------ 80 ------ 90 ------ 100

⅄

Traveler's checklist:

* **Standard firearms ownership:** unrestricted, but permit required for handgun sales
* **Semi-auto gun / high capacity magazines:** import of *assault weapons* prohibited; transfer or sale of over 10 shot magazines prohibited
* **Machine gun ownership:** state registration; otherwise compliance with federal law
* **Firearm law uniformity:** preemption law with notable exceptions, see below
* **Right of Self-Defense:** no NRA-model castle doctrine, *duty to retreat* in public areas
* **Open carry:** prohibited in all public areas unless one possesses a Maryland permit
* **Concealed carry:** license required; granted on a discretionary basis; no reciprocity for carry permits from other states
* **Vehicle carry for non-permittees:** loaded, readily accessible handguns prohibited; exceptions exist for unloaded transport; rifles & shotguns must remain unloaded
* **State Parks:** possession and carry of firearms prohibited except at designated ranges
* **Restaurants serving alcohol:** permittees may carry while eating in dining areas – see p.3
* **Duty to notify LEO of permit status:** upon demand of police officer
* **Vehicle gun possession at colleges:** subject to college administrative policy

Maryland has a multitude of restrictions on the possession of handguns and military pattern semi-autos (assault weapons). The state requires handgun purchasers to be licensed. Any firearm classified as an "assault weapon" is banned from import entirely. And the sale or transfer of any over 10 shot magazine is prohibited. Handgun carry is similarly regulated so that it is almost impossible for an unlicensed person to carry a handgun legally.

Maryland permittees: The state requires a license to carry a loaded handgun on one's person or in a vehicle. The state police issue such permits on a highly discretionary basis to persons demonstrating a *compelling need* for a 2-year term. Maryland will issue permits to nonresidents on rare occasions. But the state will not recognize carry permits from other states.

Persons without Maryland permits: A traveler without a Maryland permit may not carry a handgun on foot or in a vehicle in a loaded or readily accessible manner. But he may transport an unloaded handgun in a secure case if he is traveling to a recognized shooting competition, bonafide gun show, hunting exercise, or some other gun-related event. Magazines may remain loaded while in a vehicle as long as they are not attached to, or inserted into, any handgun. Travelers passing through the state may transport inaccessible handguns even if they are not traveling to one of these events. The weapons must be unloaded, cased and, either stowed in the trunk, or locked in a case if the vehicle has no trunk.

All Persons: Rifles and shotguns may be transported in a vehicle for any reason. But, due to Maryland's conservation/hunting laws, the weapons must be unloaded and secured in commercial cases or gun racks regardless of whether one has a Maryland permit.

Maryland's preemption statute provides uniformity for some gun laws throughout the state. But localities may still regulate the discharge of firearms within their limits and the carry of firearms within 100 yards of schools, parks, churches, public buildings, and places of public assembly. A recently enacted self-defense law provides homeowners with civil immunity from damages sustained by unlawful intruders against whom the homeowner employs deadly force.

*** 30 ***

Massachusetts

Total prohibition *(+0, the Sons of Liberty wouldn't recognize this place today)* **Total freedom**

0 ------ 10 ------ 20 ------ 30 ------ 40 ------ 50 ------ 60 ------ 70 ------ 80 ------ 90 ------ 100

Traveler's checklist:
- ***Standard firearms ownership:** restricted, permit required to possess
- ***Semi-auto / high capacity magazines:** restricted, permit required to possess (any assault weapon or over 10 shot magazine made after 9/13/1994 is prohibited)
- ***Machine gun ownership:** restricted, state permit required & federal compliance
- ***Firearm law uniformity:** firearm laws are uniformly strict throughout the state
- ***Right of Self-Defense:** no NRA-model castle doctrine, *duty to retreat* in public areas
- ***Open carry:** prohibited in all public areas unless one possesses a Massachusetts permit
- ***Concealed carry:** license issued on a discretionary basis; limited reciprocity for non-residents with carry permits from certain other states (see below)
- ***Vehicle carry by non-permittees:** handgun carry generally prohibited; standard rifles and shotguns must be unloaded and securely cased
- ***State Parks:** concealed handgun carry by Massachusetts licensees permitted
- ***Restaurants serving alcohol:** permittees may carry while eating in dining areas – see p.3
- ***Duty to notify LEO of permit status:** upon demand of police officer
- ***Vehicle gun possession at colleges:** prohibited by law

Unfortunately for gun owners, Massachusetts reflects Ted Kennedy's politics when it comes to laws regulating firearms. Mere possession of rifles, shotguns, handguns and ammunition requires a firearm identification card. And any violation of a Massachusetts' firearm law could carry a minimum sentence of one year in prison for the violator.

Massachusetts permittees: A permit is needed to carry a concealed handgun in your vehicle or on your person while on foot. Such licenses are issued to Massachusetts' residents who are 21 or older for 6-year terms on a highly discretionary basis. The state will issue temporary licenses to carry handguns to nonresidents who have carry permits from their home states. These permits cost $100.00, are valid for one year and may be obtained through the Firearms Records Bureau (617-660-4782). Any permittee in a vehicle must carry his handgun so that it is under his "exclusive" control and not in the possession of a non-permitted passenger.

Massachusetts will only recognize the carry permits of other states if the issuing state has criteria for issuance that are in accordance with Massachusetts' standards. The permittee must also be traveling to a recognized firearm competition or engaged in lawful hunting with a state hunting license. Massachusetts does not publish a list of states that they recognize in this regard.

Persons without Massachusetts permits: Vehicle carry of a handgun without a Massachusetts carry license is prohibited. Handguns may only be transported by travelers who are "passing through" the state under the provisions of McClure-Volkmer (see p 5.)

Nonresidents traveling into or through the state may transport standard rifles and shotguns in a vehicle's trunk or passenger compartment if the items are unloaded and enclosed in cases. Nonresident hunters may also possess rifles and shotguns if they have valid nonresident hunting licenses. But possession of most "large capacity" rifles and shotguns deemed to be assault weapons by state authorities requires a temporary license.

All Persons: All semi-automatic "assault weapons" and over 10 shot magazines made after 1994 are permanently banned from entering the state. And any licensee allowed to possess large capacity long guns must have them unloaded and *locked* in cases while in a vehicle.

Michigan

Total prohibition   *(+0, a fair state, unless you're a nonresident w/o a license)*   **Total freedom**

0 ------ 10 ------ 20 ------ 30 ------ 40 ------ 50 ------ 60 ------ 70 ------ 80 ------ 90 ------ 100

Traveler's checklist:

- ***Standard firearms ownership:** handgun registration required at time of purchase
- ***Semi-auto / high capacity magazines:** some folding stock carbines require NFA regstr.
- ***Machine gun ownership:** no state restrictions, compliance with federal law only
- ***Firearm law uniformity:** preemption law, firearm laws uniform throughout state
- ***Right of Self-Defense:** NRA model-castle doctrine, *stand your ground* in public areas
- ***Open carry:** unrestricted under state law, but uncommon except in rural areas
- ***Concealed carry:** licenses granted on a "shall issue" basis; automatic recognition for travelers with carry permits issued by their home states
- ***Vehicle carry by non-permittees:** long guns must be transported unloaded and encased or secured in the trunk; a nonresident may only carry a handgun in a vehicle if he has a carry license from his home state
- ***State Parks:** concealed handgun carry by recognized licensees permitted
- ***Restaurants serving alcohol:** permittees may carry while eating in dining areas – see p.3
- ***Duty to notify LEO of permit status:** immediately upon official contact
- ***Vehicle gun possession at colleges:** lawful for permittees, except at UM & WSU

Michigan's rustic northern regions serve as a draw for many gun enthusiasts. Unfortunately, Michigan's laws regulating firearms transport and carry are stricter than one might expect and should cause the unlicensed traveler concern.

Recognized permittees: Michigan requires a license to carry a handgun concealed on your person or within your vehicle. Such permits are issued through the licensing boards of an applicant's home county for five-year terms. These licenses are only available to Michigan residents and exempt the holders from having to obtain a purchase permit on subsequent pistol purchases. A nonresident with a carry permit issued by his home state may carry a loaded pistol in most public areas except sports arenas, large entertainment facilities, churches, hospitals, bars, casinos, daycare centers and universities. Parking lots of these areas (except casinos) are exempt.

When stopped by a police officer, a recognized permittee must immediately disclose that he has a concealed pistol on his person and a recognized carry license. Failure to do so can result in a fine and seizure of his handgun by authorities.

Persons without recognized permits: Michigan residents without carry permits may transport handguns for a "lawful purpose" that are securely cased, unloaded and either stored in the trunk or placed in an area that is not readily accessible to the vehicle's occupants. "Lawful purpose" includes transportation of the pistol to locations where the pistol may be employed for most recreational endeavors. The pistol's owner must have also registered the pistol with the Michigan State police when he acquired the pistol. This requirement makes it impossible for a nonresident to transport a pistol in Michigan unless he has a carry permit from his home state.

Michigan allows the open carry of a loaded pistol while one is on foot. A traveler should keep his pistol in a visible holster and take care not to enter a vehicle unless he has a carry permit.

All Persons: Long guns (rifles and shotguns) must be unloaded and at least one of the following: (1) broken down, (2) enclosed in a case, (3) placed in the trunk or, (4) inaccessible from the vehicle's interior to be legally transported in a vehicle. A perusal of case law indicates that individuals have been prosecuted for having just one live round in a rifle stored in the trunk.

Minnesota

Total prohibition *(+0, room for improvement, nonpermittees still have it tough)* **Total freedom**

0 ------ 10 ------ 20 ------ 30 ------ 40 ------ 50 ------ 60 ------ 70 ------ 80 ------ 90 ------ 100

Traveler's checklist:

* **Standard firearms ownership:** no license required (except for handgun purchases)
* **Semi-auto / high capacity magazines:** no restrictions on possession
* **Machine gun ownership:** restrictive, only machine guns which have been declared curio and relics may be possessed by individuals
* **Firearm law uniformity:** state preemption law, firearm laws uniform throughout state
* **Right of Self-Defense:** no NRA-model castle doctrine, *duty to retreat* in public areas
* **Open carry:** prohibited in all public areas unless one possesses a recognized permit
* **Concealed carry:** licenses granted on a shall issue basis to residents and non-residents; reciprocity for carry permits from certain other states (p. 65)
* **Vehicle carry by non-permittees:** handguns must be securely cased and unloaded; rifles and shotguns must always remain cased and unloaded
* **State Parks:** concealed handgun carry by recognized licensees permitted
* **Restaurants serving alcohol:** permittees may carry while eating in dining areas – see p.3
* **Duty to notify LEO of permit status:** upon demand of police officer
* **Vehicle gun possession at colleges:** lawful for any gun owner

Minnesota's numerous restrictions on the purchase and sale of handguns and "assault weapons" should not concern the casual traveler. But persons visiting America's north central region should be aware of certain legal nuances to ensure an uneventful trip.

Recognized permittees: Minnesota requires a license to carry a loaded handgun on one's person or in a vehicle. The state will grant such permits on a shall issue basis to residents and nonresidents who are at least 21 years old. Application is made to the county sheriff of the resident's home county. Non-residents may apply to any sheriff in the state. Permits are valid for five years and allow concealed or open carry. Out-of-state permits from "substantially similar" states are recognized at the discretion of the Commissioner of Public Safety. Aside from some universally restricted areas (p.6), most public venues are open to carry by permittees. But private establishments that post signs and public institutions, such as universities, which enforce internal policies against carry are off-limits. Such places can only prohibit carry within buildings and, with the exception of churches, may not restrict possession in parking facilities.

Persons without recognized permits: Handguns in a vehicle must be unloaded and fully contained in closed commercial gun cases. The weapons may be transported in either the passenger compartment or trunk but must always remain unloaded and cased.

While on foot, handguns may be transported between one's premises and place of business without a permit. Persons engaged in lawful hunting and target shooting may also carry handguns without permits while engaged in these pursuits. Aside from these few exceptions, carrying a loaded handgun in public without a license is not allowed.

All Persons: Rifles and shotguns in a vehicle must be unloaded and secured in commercial gun cases unless stowed in the trunk. Long guns in a vehicle's trunk must be unloaded but need not be cased. This restriction applies to permittees and non-permittees alike because Minnesota's licensing law only allows for *handgun* carry with a permit. Open carry of long guns while on foot is limited to lawful hunting or target shooting pursuits. Any other possession in public areas would require that the weapons be unloaded and secured in gun cases.

Mississippi

Total prohibition *(+3, better preemption makes this state one of our best)* **Total freedom**

0 ------ 10 ------ 20 ------ 30 ------ 40 ------ 50 ------ 60 ------ 70 ------ 80 ------ 90 ------ 100

Traveler's checklist:

* **Standard firearms ownership:** unrestricted, no permit or license required
* **Semi-auto / high capacity magazines:** no restrictions on possession or sale
* **Machine gun ownership:** no state restrictions, compliance with federal law only
* **Firearm law uniformity:** preemption law, but cities may restrict parks & public meetings
* **Right of Self-Defense:** NRA-model castle doctrine, *stand your ground* in public areas
* **Open carry:** unrestricted under state law in most public areas (local restrictions possible)
* **Concealed carry:** licenses granted to residents on a "shall issue" basis; automatic recognition of carry permits from all other states
* **Vehicle carry by non-permittees:** loaded, concealed handguns may be carried anywhere in a vehicle; long guns should be unloaded during hunting season
* **State Parks:** concealed handgun carry by recognized licensees permitted
* **Restaurants serving alcohol:** permittees may carry while eating in dining areas – see p.3
* **Duty to notify LEO of permit status:** upon demand of police officer
* **Vehicle gun possession at colleges:** lawful for any non-student gun owner

Mississippi's rural character provides the gun-owning traveler with some very scenic highway driving as well as relatively unrestrictive firearm laws. The National Rifle Association has been instrumental in helping to pass pro-gun legislation in the state's General Assembly. These laws ensure that the nonresident gun owner will have a pleasant visit to the Magnolia State.

Recognized permittees: A license is required to carry a concealed handgun while on foot. Such permits are granted to residents for 5-year terms and may be upgraded to "enhanced" status through additional training. This would allow the enhanced permittee to carry in most prohibited areas. Mississippi does not issue licenses to nonresidents but will recognize carry permits from all other states. Permittees may carry openly or concealed.

Carry for regular permittees is prohibited at most athletic events, colleges, bars, churches, parades, polling places and any business or private establishment that posts a sign against carry.

Persons without recognized permits: A license is not required to carry a loaded, concealed handgun in a vehicle. Glove compartments, console boxes, briefcases, gym bags, or under the seat are legitimate areas for stowage.

Firearm may be carried openly while on foot as long as they are not "hidden or obscured from common observation." A pistol carried in a sheath or belt holster is O.K. as long as the holster or sheath is visible. Firearms may also be concealed while on foot if one is involved in "legitimate weapons-related activities" such as target shooting, hunting, or fishing.

All Persons: Standard length rifles and shotguns are not affected by Mississippi's concealed weapons statute. Persons on foot may carry such weapons in most public areas and just about anywhere in a vehicle with one important qualification. Hunting laws require long guns in a vehicle, or possessed on foot while one is on a public road or highway, to be unloaded during deer and turkey season. Such weapons may be loaded during other times of the year. This prohibition applies to both permittees and non-permittees. Also, businesses may only prohibit firearms inside their buildings. Guns kept in locked vehicles on their parking lots are lawful.

Localities may only restrict carry in certain areas such as public parks and meetings. The strengthened preemption law sets legal sanctions against cities that attempt overbroad regulation.

Missouri

Total prohibition *(+3, open carry preemption for licensees, Show Me state rocks!)* **Total freedom**

0 ------ 10 ------ 20 ------ 30 ------ 40 ------ 50 ------ 60 ------ 70 ------ 80 ------ 90 ------ 100

Traveler's checklist:

*Standard firearms ownership: unrestricted, no permit or license required

*Semi-auto / high capacity magazines: no restrictions on possession or sale

*Machine gun ownership: no state restrictions, compliance with federal law only

*Firearm law uniformity: preemption law, gun laws uniform except localities may regulate the open carry of loaded weapons by non-permittees in public areas

*Right of Self-Defense: NRA-model castle doctrine, *stand your ground* limited to vehicle

*Open carry: unrestricted under state law; some local regulation of loaded carry is possible

*Concealed carry: licenses granted on a "shall issue" basis; automatic recognition for travelers with carry permits from other states

*Vehicle carry by non-permittees: concealed, loaded handguns may be carried anywhere in a vehicle by persons 19 years of age or older; loaded rifles and shotguns must be transported in plain view

*State Parks: concealed handgun carry by recognized licensees permitted

*Restaurants serving alcohol: permittees may carry while eating in dining areas – see p.3

*Duty to notify LEO of permit status: upon demand of police officer

*Vehicle gun possession at colleges: lawful for permittees, but subject to college policy

Missouri developed a well-earned reputation during the Civil War as a place where personal gun ownership was a necessity for survival. With roving bands of soldiers from both sides exacting a heavy toll on the population, farmers in the hinterland needed plenty of firepower just to stay alive. Missourians continue this tradition today with laws friendly to gun ownership.

Recognized permittees: Missouri issues concealed carry licenses to qualified residents who are at least 19 years old on a "shall issue" basis through the applicant's local sheriff. The licenses are valid for five years and allow the carry of any firearm. Missouri does not issue permits to non-residents but will recognize any carry permit issued by another state or locality. Recognized permittees may carry openly or concealed in most public areas. But certain places are off-limits. Large sports arenas, amusement parks, churches, colleges, hospitals, casinos, bars, and posted private establishments prohibit carry. These restrictions only apply to the buildings of such places. Weapons secured in vehicles in parking lots are lawful.

Persons without recognized permits: Any person 19 years or older (or 18 years if member of the military) may carry a loaded, concealed handgun in a vehicle. The weapon can be located anywhere within the passenger compartment or trunk. A handgun carried in the glove compartment, console box or gym bag is legitimate as long as the weapon remains within the vehicle and the person's possession of the firearm is otherwise lawful. Non-military persons under 19 should transport their handguns unloaded, cased and separate from any ammunition unless they possess valid carry permits. Rifles and shotguns may be carried loaded and in plain view. If the weapons are concealed from view, they should be unloaded and secured in cases.

Open carry on foot is allowed in most public areas with one notable exception. Cities may prohibit the open carry of loaded firearms by anyone without a license. Local ordinances exist which prohibit any non-permittee from having an openly displayed, loaded gun in public.

All Persons: Missouri has a strong preemption law that prevents most local regulation of firearm issues. But, be aware, that state law prohibits gun possession by anyone on a bus.

Montana

Total prohibition   *(+0, Big Sky lives up to its gun friendly reputation)*   **Total freedom**

0 ------ 10 ------ 20 ------ 30 ------ 40 ------ 50 ------ 60 ------ 70 ------ 80 ------ 90 ------ 100

Λ

Traveler's checklist:

*   **Standard firearms ownership:** unrestricted, no permit or license required
*   **Semi-auto / high capacity magazines:** no restrictions on possession or sale
*   **Machine gun ownership:** no state restrictions, compliance with federal law only
*   **Firearm law uniformity:** preemption law, some local regulation of public areas possible
*   **Right of Self-Defense:** NRA-model castle doctrine, *stand your ground* in public areas
*   **Open carry:** unrestricted in most public areas and generally accepted
*   **Concealed carry:** licenses granted on a "shall issue" basis; reciprocity available for travelers with carry permits from certain other states (see p. 65)
*   **Vehicle carry by non-permittees:** loaded firearms may be carried in plain view, console box, glove compartment or commercial gun case; firearms may not be concealed *on one's person* in a vehicle (see below)
*   **State Parks:** concealed handgun carry by recognized licensees permitted
*   **Restaurants serving alcohol:** concealed carry prohibited for everyone
*   **Duty to notify LEO of permit status:** upon demand of police officer
*   **Vehicle gun possession at colleges:** subject to college administrative policy

Montana's vast expanse offers the traveler some breathtaking views as well as ample incentive to carry a firearm for personal protection. The state's historical connections to the "Old West" are vividly reflected in its firearm laws.

Recognized permittees: The state requires a license to carry a concealed weapon within the boundaries of most population centers. The sheriff of an applicant's home county issues permits to qualified residents 18 years or older for four-year terms. Montana does not grant licenses to nonresidents but will recognize the permits of other states under certain conditions. The state that issued the permit must require a background check of applicants prior to permit issuance. And the nonresident permittee must also possess photo identification along with his actual permit if the permit itself has no photo. Recognized permittees can carry concealed in most public areas. Notable exceptions include government buildings, banks & financial institutions, bars, and restaurants serving alcohol.

Persons without recognized permits: Montana allows anyone to carry a concealed firearm when they are outside the boundary of a city, town or logging camp. Persons engaged in outdoor activities such as hiking and camping may also carry concealed firearms without permits.

"Concealed" in Montana is defined as "carrying or bearing concealed upon one's person" a deadly weapon that is "wholly or partially covered by wearing apparel." Absent one of the exceptions noted in the previous paragraph, wearing a handgun under your outer clothing would be illegal. But if the weapon is in plain view or secured from view in such a way as not to be "on your person," the carry of the loaded firearm would be legitimate. In a vehicle, a loaded handgun could be placed in a console box, glove compartment or under one's seat. A long gun could be kept in a gun case or gun rack. Trunk transport would also be acceptable.

All Persons: Open carry is generally accepted and supported by statute. The areas listed as "off-limits" to licensed concealed carry are actually O.K. for open carry. But localities may still prohibit any gun carry in public parks, buildings, and assemblies. And even though carry on trains is prohibited to everyone, hotels may not prohibit guests from possessing firearms.

Nebraska

Total prohibition   *(+0, improved, but still tough for non-permittee travel)*   **Total freedom**

0 ------ 10 ------ 20 ------ 30 ------ 40 ------ 50 ------ 60 ------ 70 ------ 80 ------ 90 ------ 100

人

Traveler's checklist:

*Standard firearms ownership: no license required (except for handgun purchases)

*Semi-auto / high capacity magazines: no restrictions on possession or sale

*Machine gun ownership: no state restrictions, compliance with federal law only

*Firearm law uniformity: preemption law, local regulation of concealed carry prohibited

*Right of Self-Defense: no NRA-model castle doctrine, *duty to retreat* in public areas

*Open carry: unrestricted under state law; some local regulation possible

*Concealed carry: licenses granted to residents on a shall issue basis; reciprocity available for nonresidents with carry permits from certain other states (see p.65)

*Vehicle carry by non-permittees: shotguns must be unloaded; rifles & handguns may be in plain view and loaded under state law, but local laws may prohibit this; to be safe, all firearms in the passenger compartment should be cased and unloaded

*State Parks: concealed handgun carry by recognized licensees permitted

*Restaurants Serving alcohol: permittees may carry while eating in dining areas – see p.3

*Duty to notify LEO of permit status: immediately upon official contact (EMS also)

*Vehicle gun possession at colleges: lawful for permittees, but subject to college policy

Nebraska is in the heart of America's breadbasket and is often a state that travelers pass through on their way to a vacation destination in the far West. Nebraska will provide recognized permittees with a relatively benign atmosphere for gun carry. But travelers without permits should be aware that, despite state preemption of issues affecting permit holders, Nebraska still allows localities to regulate firearms carry and possession by non-licensees.

Recognized permittees: Nebraska requires a license to carry a concealed handgun in a vehicle or on or about one's person. The State Patrol issues such permits to any Nebraska resident who is at least 21 years old and a U.S. citizen. Licenses are valid for five years, cost $100.00 and are for handgun carry only. Nebraska recognizes out-of-state licenses from states that have equal or greater issuance standards. Recognized permittees may not be residents of Nebraska and must be at least 21 years old. When approached by a police officer or EMS, a permittee must declare that he is carrying a concealed handgun. Places off-limits to carry include banks, churches, athletic events, colleges, hospitals, political rallies, and any posted business. Parking lot possession is exempted from these restrictions if the gun stays locked in the vehicle.

Persons without recognized permits: Concealed carry of a loaded handgun is prohibited either in a vehicle or while a person is on foot. Loaded handguns in a vehicle should be stowed in the trunk. A handgun that is *unloaded* may be kept in a closed commercial gun case inside the vehicle. But loaded handguns that are hidden from view and readily accessible (ie. under the seat or in an unlocked glove compartment) are illegal. While on foot, the handgun must be in a visible belt holster and not be in violation of a local ordinance prohibiting open carry. Affirmative defenses to a charge of carrying concealed exist. A traveler who can prove the necessity of carry for self-defense may successfully defend against a conviction.

All Persons: Loaded rifles in a vehicle must be in plain view or cased and kept in the passenger compartment or trunk. Shotguns transported in a vehicle must be unloaded and may be in plain view or enclosed in gun cases. Nebraska's concealed carry law only applies to handgun carry. Permittees and non-permittees must observe the same rules for long gun transport.

Nevada

Total prohibition   (*+0, good gun state, but local laws linger in Clark County*)   **Total freedom**

0 ------ 10 ------ 20 ------ 30 ------ 40 ------ 50 ------ 60 ------ 70 ------ 80 ------ 90 ------ 100

Traveler's checklist:

> ***Standard firearms ownership:** unrestricted, no permit or license required by state
>
> ***Semi-auto gun / high capacity magazines:** no restrictions on possession or sale
>
> ***Machine gun ownership:** no state restrictions, compliance with federal law only
>
> ***Firearm law uniformity:** preemption law; laws mostly uniform, some local ordinances enacted prior to 1989 continue to be enforced in parts of Clark County
>
> ***Right of Self-Defense:** NRA-model castle doctrine, *stand your ground* in public areas
>
> ***Open carry:** unrestricted under state law; some cities may still *attempt* to regulate this
>
> ***Concealed carry:** licenses granted on a "shall issue" basis to qualified persons; reciprocity available for nonresidents with carry permits from certain other states (see p. 65)
>
> ***Vehicle carry by non-permittees:** rifles and shotguns carried in a vehicle must be "unloaded;" handguns may be carried openly or in the glove compartment but may not be concealed upon one's person
>
> ***State Parks:** concealed handgun carry by recognized licensees permitted
>
> ***Restaurants serving alcohol:** permittees may carry while eating in dining areas – see p.3
>
> ***Duty to notify LEO of permit status:** upon demand of police officer
>
> ***Vehicle gun possession at colleges:** prohibited by law absent written permission

Much of Nevada is open country with Las Vegas and Reno being the only sizable urban centers. This provides a political atmosphere that is generally friendly for gun ownership. Travelers should experience no problems if they are mindful of several important points.

Recognized permittees: Nevada issues licenses to carry concealed firearms to residents and nonresidents who are at least 21 years old. A resident must apply to his local sheriff while a nonresident may apply to any county sheriff. Licenses are valid for five years. Nevada will also recognize carry permits of nonresidents from states with similar laws. Recognized permittees may carry concealed firearms anywhere in the state except most universally restricted areas (see p.6), universities, secure facilities, public airports and posted public buildings.

Persons without recognized permits: A traveler may possess a loaded handgun in a vehicle's passenger compartment if the weapon is in plain view or secured in the glove compartment or console box. A handgun may not be concealed "upon one's person." A weapon hidden under one's clothing or in a container carried by the person would be illegal. But a loaded handgun secured in a gun case on an empty passenger seat would be legitimate.

On foot, a non-permittee may carry a handgun openly as long as the weapon is in a visible holster. This carry mode is common in rural areas but unlikely to be seen in Las Vegas.

All Persons: Vehicle carry of rifles and shotguns is allowed as long as the firearms are unloaded and not concealed on one's person. "Unloaded" in Nevada is defined as a firearm that has no live cartridge in the firing chamber. Magazines for rifles and shotguns may remain loaded. This restriction applies to both permittees and non-permittees.

Nevada's preemption law prohibits localities from enacting laws regulating transportation, ownership, sale, and possession of firearms. Some cities continue to enforce local carry ordinances passed before 1989. Travelers should be aware that, despite the apparent invalidity of these enforcements, violations could still result in arrests. Also, resident handgun registration in Clark County only applies to residents and does not affect visitors to the area.

New Hampshire

Total prohibition   *(+0, freedom & firearms, who said Yankees don't like guns?)*   **Total freedom**

0 ------ 10 ------ 20 ------ 30 ------ 40 ------ 50 ------ 60 ------ 70 ------ 80 ------ 90 ------ 100

Traveler's checklist:

*   ***Standard firearms ownership:*** unrestricted, no permit or license required
*   ***Semi-auto / high capacity magazines:*** no restrictions on possession or sale
*   ***Machine gun ownership:*** no state restrictions, compliance with federal law only
*   ***Firearm law uniformity:*** preemption law; firearm laws uniform throughout the state
*   ***Right of Self-Defense:*** NRA-model castle doctrine, *stand your ground* in public areas
*   ***Open carry:*** unrestricted under state law and generally accepted
*   ***Concealed carry:*** "shall issue" licenses granted; reciprocity available for nonresidents with carry permits from their home states (see p. 65); nonresidents may also apply for in-state carry permits.
*   ***Vehicle carry by non-permittees:*** handguns must be unloaded and may be carried openly or secured in gun cases in the passenger compartment; rifles & shotguns must be unloaded while in a vehicle
*   ***State Parks:*** concealed handgun carry by recognized licensees permitted
*   ***Restaurants serving alcohol:*** permittees may carry while eating in dining areas – see p.3
*   ***Duty to notify LEO of permit status:*** upon demand of police officer
*   ***Vehicle gun possession at colleges:*** subject to college administrative policy

Citizens of New Hampshire are proud of their state's dedication to personal liberties. New Hampshire's motto, "Live Free or Die," illustrates how strongly the state supports the ideas of the founding fathers through its legal treatment of firearms. Despite its geographical location in the restrictive northeast, the "Granite State" reflects the best in American constitutional values.

Recognized permittees: A license is required to carry a loaded handgun in a vehicle or concealed upon one's person. The police chief or sheriff of a resident's hometown issues such a permit for a 4-year term. Permits are also issued to nonresidents through the state police. Nonresident permits cost $100.00 and require the applicant to have a carry permit from his home state. New Hampshire will recognize permits from states that also recognize New Hampshire if the permittee is a resident of the state issuing the permit. Permittees may carry in most public areas except courthouses and posted property.

Persons without recognized permits: Vehicle carry of a handgun is limited to a weapon that is unloaded. An unloaded handgun may be carried openly or secured in a gun case, glove compartment or console box. Detached magazines may remain loaded as long as they are not inserted into the handgun. New Hampshire only prohibits the carry of a *loaded* handgun in a vehicle without a license. The position of the weapon is not regulated. So an unloaded handgun, with an unattached, loaded magazine nearby, can be carried just about anywhere in a vehicle.

Open carry of a loaded handgun while on foot is allowed in most public areas except courthouses and posted private property. A concealed, *unloaded* handgun may be carried with a loaded magazine as long as the magazine is not inserted in the weapon. New Hampshire's preemption law prevents localities from regulating this and most other aspects of gun ownership.

All Persons: Rifles and shotguns in a vehicle must be unloaded and should be kept in gun cases, gun racks, or trunks. Loaded magazines for these weapons may be carried if they are not attached to any firearm. New Hampshire only authorizes handgun carry by persons with recognized licenses. Long gun transport is the same for both permittees and non-permittees.

New Jersey

Total prohibition   *(+0, a good example of how bad things can truly become)*   **Total freedom**

0 ------ 10 ------ 20 ------ 30 ------ 40 ------ 50 ------ 60 ------ 70 ------ 80 ------ 90 ------ 100

Traveler's checklist:

- ***Standard firearms ownership:** restricted, carry permit needed for handgun possession unless exception applies; purchaser identification card required for long guns
- ***Semi-auto / high capacity magazines:** highly restricted, all firearms deemed "assault weapons" and any over 15 shot magazines are banned from entering the state
- ***Machine gun ownership:** individual ownership of machine guns is prohibited
- ***Firearm law uniformity:** firearm laws are strict, no state preemption
- ***Right of Self-Defense:** no NRA-model castle doctrine, *duty to retreat* in public areas
- ***Open carry:** prohibited in all public areas unless one has a New Jersey carry permit
- ***Concealed carry:** licenses issued on a highly discretionary basis; no reciprocity for other state permits; but New Jersey will issue permits to non-residents
- ***Vehicle carry by non-permittees:** firearms may not be carried in a vehicle without a purchaser identification card or NJ carry permit
- ***State Parks:** firearms possession or use prohibited
- ***Restaurants serving alcohol:** permittees may carry while eating in dining areas – see p.3
- ***Duty to notify LEO of permit status:** upon demand of police officer
- ***Vehicle gun possession at colleges:** prohibited by law

Travelers to New Jersey should be prepared for highly restrictive firearm laws. The state's urban demographics and left-wing political bent have made it a hell house for gun owners.

New Jersey permittees: New Jersey requires a license to carry a loaded handgun on your person or in a vehicle. New Jersey residents may apply to their local police chief for such a permit. Non-residents must apply directly to the Superintendent of State Police. Such licenses are then issued by a state Superior court for a two-year term and are granted on a highly discretionary basis. The state does not recognize any out-of-state permits. Citizens have found it almost impossible to obtain a New Jersey carry permit absent a "compelling" need.

Persons without New Jersey permits: Handgun possession outside of one's home or business generally requires a carry permit issued by a New Jersey Superior court. Rifle and shotgun possession requires a firearm purchaser identification card issued by a person's local police chief or by the state police if the applicant is an out-of-state resident. A card or permit is also required for vehicle transport of these firearms. Strict exceptions to this prohibition allow the transport of unloaded and securely cased firearms without a card or permit if a person is traveling directly to a hunting engagement, firearms exhibition, repair facility or target range. But general transport within the state is prohibited. Travelers lacking an identification card or failing to qualify for an exception should leave all firearms at home unless transporting per p.5.

Open carry of a handgun without a New Jersey license is strictly prohibited. New Jersey does not differentiate between open or concealed carry. Both carry modes are prohibited unless one is engaged in hunting or shooting activity in an area officially sanctioned for such pursuit.

All Persons: Personal ownership of military-pattern semi-automatic weapons, over 15 shot magazines, machine guns and most hollow point handgun ammo is prohibited. Travelers should take care to leave all such items behind when traveling to New Jersey. An exception exists for residents to keep hollow point ammunition in their homes. But importation of such ammunition by nonresident travelers is prohibited.

New Mexico

Total prohibition   *(+0, southwestern sensibility rules when it comes to guns)*   **Total freedom**

0 ------ 10 ------ 20 ------ 30 ------ 40 ------ 50 ------ 60 ------ 70 ------ 80 ------ 90 ------ 100

Traveler's checklist:

* **Standard firearms ownership:** unrestricted, no permit or license required
* **Semi-auto gun / high capacity magazines:** no restrictions on possession or sale
* **Machine gun ownership:** no state restrictions, compliance with federal law only
* **Firearm law uniformity:** preemption law, firearm laws uniform throughout state
* **Right of Self-Defense:** no NRA castle doctrine, *stand your ground* in public not codified
* **Open carry:** unrestricted in most public areas and generally accepted
* **Concealed carry:** licenses granted to residents on a shall issue basis; reciprocity available for carry permits from certain other states (see p. 65)
* **Vehicle carry by non-permittees:** loaded, concealed firearms may be carried anywhere in a private automobile for self-protection
* **State Parks:** concealed handgun carry by recognized licensees permitted
* **Restaurants serving alcohol:** permittees allowed to carry with qualification (see below)
* **Duty to notify LEO of permit status:** upon demand of police officer
* **Vehicle gun possession at colleges:** lawful for anyone over 19, subject to college policy

New Mexico was named the "Land of Enchantment" for its rugged mountain terrain and vast prairie tracts. Gun ownership has always been an important part of life for New Mexicans. As late as 1916, citizens in the southern border town of Columbus used their privately owned arms to repel an attack by Mexican bandit Pancho Villa. This incident illustrates the well-established historical imperative for gun ownership in this frontier state of the Southwest.

Recognized permittees: New Mexico requires a license to carry a loaded, concealed handgun while on foot. Licenses are issued to residents on a "shall issue" basis through the Department of Public Safety and are granted for four-year terms to persons 21 years or older. New Mexico will not issue permits to nonresidents but will recognize permits from other states that have reciprocity agreements with New Mexico. A recognized permittee is limited to carrying only one handgun at a time. He must also be a U.S. citizen and at least 21 years old. Carry is prohibited on any "posted" property as well as on tribal lands, colleges and courthouses. Permittees can carry in restaurants that serve beer and wine but not ones that serve hard liquor.

Persons without recognized permits: Vehicle carry of firearms is unrestricted. Loaded, concealed firearms may be carried in the passenger compartment or trunk. Under the seat, in the glove compartment or concealed in a purse are all legitimate placement areas.

A non-permittee on foot can similarly carry an *unloaded* firearm anywhere on his person. The weapon can be concealed from view in a snapped belt holster or secured in a commercial gun case. Loaded handguns can be openly carried on foot in most public places. One area off-limits to such carry and, of most importance to the traveler, is any retail establishment that sells, distributes or serves alcohol. Loaded or unloaded carry in these areas is punishable as a felony unless one has a recognized permit or fits into a statutory exception.

All Persons: Open or concealed carry is prohibited to all persons on public buses, game preserves, university campuses, schools, courthouses and restaurants that serve hard liquor. Any local ordinances that might create even more restricted areas are rendered non-issues by New Mexico's strong preemption law. But 18 year olds from other states should be aware that handgun possession is limited to persons 19 years and older.

New York

Total prohibition   *(+2, 7 round limit on magazine capacity overturned by court)*   **Total freedom**

0 ------ 10 ------ 20 ------ 30 ------ 40 ------ 50 ------ 60 ------ 70 ------ 80 ------ 90 ------ 100

λ

Traveler's checklist:

* **Standard firearms ownership:** restricted, permit required for handgun possession; no license required for rifle or shotgun possession
* **Semi-auto gun / high capacity magazines:** restricted; "assault weapons" (semi-auto military-style replicas) and magazines over 10 shots may not be imported
* **Machine gun ownership:** personal ownership of machine guns prohibited
* **Firearm law uniformity:** some local regulation, especially in New York City
* **Right of Self-Defense:** no NRA-model castle doctrine, *duty to retreat* in public areas
* **Open carry:** prohibited in all public areas
* **Concealed carry:** licenses granted on a highly discretionary basis; no reciprocity for travelers with carry permits from other states
* **Vehicle carry for non-permittees:** rifles and shotguns must be unloaded; handgun possession or carry requires a New York license
* **State Parks:** firearm possession or use prohibited
* **Restaurants serving alcohol:** permittees may carry while eating in dining areas – see p.3
* **Duty to notify LEO of permit status:** upon demand of police officer
* **Vehicle gun possession at colleges:** prohibited by law

New York is typical of many eastern seaboard states in that licensing and registration of firearms have been well established for decades. Since 1911, mere possession of a handgun by a New York resident, even in one's own home, requires a New York license to possess or carry.

New York permittees: New York requires a license to possess or carry a handgun. Such permits are issued to residents on a discretionary basis through their home county. If the license has no stated restrictions, the permittee may carry the handgun loaded and concealed. Open carry is not allowed for anyone, including licensees. New York does not issue licenses to nonresidents unless the person is *principally employed* within the state (ie. bank guards) or lives in New York part-time. And New York will not honor out-of-state permits. This makes handgun carry by the out-of-state traveler, either in a vehicle or on one's person, nearly impossible.

Persons without New York permits: A traveler wishing to transport his handgun through the state may do so if the weapon is unloaded and secured in a locked case in the trunk or storage area. The traveler's ultimate destination must also be a state where unlicensed possession is permitted. Any extended stops in New York would render the "through" nature of the trip void and thus subject the traveler to prosecution by state authorities. A traveler should carry proof of hotel reservations in his destination state to prove the interstate nature of his trip.

All Persons: Anyone may transport standard rifles and shotguns into New York without a license as long as the weapons are unloaded and secured in commercial gun cases. Long guns in a vehicle must be unloaded even if one possesses a New York pistol permit. Machine guns, semi-automatic *assault weapons* and over 10 shot magazines are prohibited from importation. A federal judge struck down a mandate that limited loaded magazine capacity to no more than (7) rounds. But the case is still being litigated. So gun owners should keep abreast of any changes.

The possession of any firearm in the City of New York without a New York City license is strictly prohibited. But persons transporting standard rifles and shotguns through the City may do so for a 24-hr. period after entering the City if the weapons are unloaded and locked in cases.

North Carolina

Total prohibition   *(+0, good state, unlicensed vehicle carry could be better)*   **Total freedom**

0 ------ 10 ------ 20 ------ 30 ------ 40 ------ 50 ------ 60 ------ 70 ------ 80 ------ 90 ------ 100

Traveler's checklist:

*   ***Standard firearms ownership:** no license required (except for handgun purchases)
*   ***Semi-auto / high capacity magazines:** no restrictions on possession or sale
*   ***Machine gun ownership:** permit from sheriff and compliance with federal law
*   ***Firearm law uniformity:** preemption law, but some local carry restrictions possible
*   ***Right of Self-Defense:** NRA-model castle doctrine, *stand your ground* in public areas
*   ***Open carry:** unrestricted under state law except for certain specified public areas
*   ***Concealed carry:** licenses granted to residents on a "shall issue" basis; automatic recognition of carry permits from all other states
*   ***Vehicle carry by non-permittees:** loaded firearms may be secured in holsters or slings and carried openly in the vehicle's passenger compartment
*   ***State Parks:** concealed handgun carry by recognized licensees permitted
*   ***Restaurants serving alcohol:** permittees may carry if premises are not "posted" – see p.3
*   ***Duty to notify LEO of permit status:** immediately upon official contact
*   ***Vehicle gun possession at colleges:** lawful for permittees, private schools may prohibit

The beautiful scenery of the Blue Ridge Mountains as well as the state's user-friendly firearm laws will impress visitors to North Carolina. The state's rural areas, in particular, provide a vivid reminder that Andy Griffith's Mayberry is alive and well in the Tar Heel state.

Recognized permittees: North Carolina issues licenses to carry concealed, loaded handguns to qualified residents 21 years or older on a "shall issue" basis through the applicant's home county sheriff for a five year term. North Carolina does not issue permits to nonresidents but will recognize permits from all other states. When approached by a police officer, a recognized permittee must declare that he has a concealed handgun with a valid permit. Permittees may carry in most public areas except state government offices, the state capitol, courts, educational properties (including colleges) and posted prohibited areas. Handguns locked in vehicles parked on government / state educational premises are exempt from this prohibition.

Persons without recognized permits: Vehicle carry of loaded handguns is limited to those weapons that are in plain view. A pistol placed in a hip holster or on the vehicle's dash or passenger seat is acceptable if the weapon remains visible from outside the vehicle. Handguns carried in *locked* glove compartments or console boxes have been deemed lawful by the state department of public safety. But the attorney general's office still discourages such carry. Travelers should be aware of this contradiction among official sources if they intend to exercise this option. Courts have held that any concealment of a readily accessible handgun in the passenger compartment could constitute carrying a concealed weapon.

Open carry of a loaded handgun while on foot is lawful in many public areas. But carry by non-permittees is still prohibited at political demonstrations, funeral processions, educational properties (including universities & colleges), picket lines, parades, public events and private establishments where alcohol is served, the state capitol and North Carolina courts.

All Persons: Loaded rifles and shotguns may be carried in racks or slings if they remain visible from outside the vehicle. Cased long guns in the storage compartment, trunk or rear-most cargo area are also acceptable. But long guns should not be concealed about one's person even if one has a recognized permit. The permit law only allows the carry of concealed handguns.

North Dakota

Total prohibition *(+0, preemption law & non-permittee carry need improvement)* **Total freedom**

0 ------ 10 ------ 20 ------ 30 ------ 40 ------ 50 ------ 60 ------ 70 ------ 80 ------ 90 ------ 100

Traveler's checklist:

*   ***Standard firearms ownership:** unrestricted, no permit or license required
*   ***Semi-auto gun / high capacity magazines:** no restrictions on possession or sale
*   ***Machine gun ownership:** no state restrictions, compliance with federal law only
*   ***Firearm law uniformity:** preemption law, local regulation of carry *not* preempted
*   ***Right of Self-Defense:** NRA-model castle doctrine, *stand your ground* in vehicle only
*   ***Open carry:** loaded carry prohibited for non-permittees; some exceptions – see below
*   ***Concealed carry:** licenses granted to qualified persons on a "shall issue" basis; reciprocity available for carry permits from certain other states (see p. 65)
*   ***Vehicle carry by non-permittees:** rifles and shotguns carried in a vehicle must be unloaded; a handgun must be unloaded and may be carried openly in a belt holster during daytime hours or hidden from view during all hours if secured in a gun case or a closed trunk
*   ***State Parks:** concealed handgun carry by recognized licensees permitted
*   ***Restaurants serving alcohol:** permittees may carry if area is open to those under 21 (p.3)
*   ***Duty to notify LEO of permit status:** upon demand of police officer
*   ***Vehicle gun possession at colleges:** lawful for anyone, but subject to policy enforcement

North Dakota's frigid winters can make one of America's northern-most states appear pretty uninviting. But the harsh climate has helped to forge a population of hardy souls that call upon firearms for daily use more often than most. This dependence on the gun has created a legal atmosphere that most gun owners will find appealing, save a few important qualifications.

Recognized permittees: North Dakota requires a license to carry a loaded firearm in a vehicle or concealed on one's person. Such permits are issued by the Bureau of Criminal Investigation to qualified persons 18 years and older for a five-year term. They are divided into Class I and Class II permits and allow the carry of any firearm. North Dakota grants permits to nonresidents and will recognize any permit issued by a state that also recognizes North Dakota.

Persons without recognized permits: A traveler without a permit may carry firearms in a vehicle if the weapons are unloaded and in plain view or properly secured. Unloaded handguns may be carried in visible belt holsters during daytime hours and secured in commercial gun cases during all hours. Glove compartment or console box carry is not permitted. But trunk or luggage compartment containment is legitimate. To be unloaded, a handgun's chamber and magazine must be void of all ammunition.

Rifles and shotguns may be in cases or secured in gun racks. Long guns need only be chamber unloaded. Their magazines may contain ammunition. If the long guns are uncased and hidden from view, they should be placed in the trunk or vehicle storage compartment.

Persons engaged in hunting and target shooting may carry loaded handguns while on foot without carry permits. Any non-permittee at a temporary residence (ie. campsite) may also carry.

All Persons: Everyone, including recognized permittees, is forbidden from carrying firearms at "public gatherings." This would include athletic events, school functions, churches (unless allowed by church), political rallies, musical concerts, and public parks (excluding state and national parks). Firearms kept within vehicles at these locations, as well as most work sites, are exempt. Gun carry in bars, casinos or gaming sites is also prohibited.

Ohio

Total prohibition *(+0, greatly improved, unlicensed vehicle carry needs work)* **Total freedom**

0 ------ 10 ------ 20 ------ 30 ------ 40 ------ 50 ------ 60 ------ 70 ------ 80 ------ 90 ------ 100

Λ

Traveler's checklist:

*   ***Standard firearms ownership:** unrestricted, no permit or license required
*   ***Semi-auto gun / high capacity magazines:** semi-autos w/ over 31 shot mag prohibited
*   ***Machine gun ownership:** safe storage required and compliance with federal law
*   ***Firearm law uniformity:** preemption law, most firearm issues regulated exclusively by state law; local weapons bans and carry restriction are unenforceable
*   ***Right of Self-Defense:** NRA-model castle doctrine, *stand your ground* in vehicle only
*   ***Open carry:** unrestricted under state law and becoming more accepted
*   ***Concealed carry:** licenses granted to residents on a shall issue basis; reciprocity available for permits issued by certain other states (see p. 65)
*   ***Vehicle carry by non-permittees:** firearms must be unloaded, the weapons must be in plain view with actions open or enclosed in cases
*   ***State Parks:** concealed handgun carry by recognized licensees in outdoor areas permitted
*   ***Restaurants serving alcohol:** permittees may carry while eating in dining areas – see p. 3
*   ***Duty to notify LEO of permit status:** immediately upon official contact
*   ***Vehicle gun possession at colleges:** lawful for permittees, but preempted policies exist

Ohio has made great improvements in its gun laws recently. These advancements are worth noting because the state is often considered a bellwether for national trends.

Recognized permittees: Ohio requires a license to carry a concealed, loaded handgun. The sheriff of a person's home county or an adjacent county will issue a license to any qualified person 21 years or older for a five-year term. Ohio will not issue licenses to nonresidents but will recognize states that recognize Ohio permits and have similar standards of issuance.

During a traffic stop, a recognized licensee must remain in his vehicle, keep his hands in plain sight and may not touch or attempt to grasp the handgun. He must also immediately inform the officer that he has a carry license with a handgun.

A permittee may not carry in colleges, churches (unless church governing body grants permission), child day care centers, gov't buildings where official business is conducted and any posted private business. But he may possess a handgun in the parking areas of colleges if the weapon remains secured in his vehicle. And most state & local government buildings that are primarily used as parking or restroom facilities are also legitimate for licensed carry.

Persons without recognized permits: Vehicle transport is limited to a weapon that is unloaded and in plain view with its actions open. The unloaded firearm may also be secured in a closed commercial gun case, gun rack or trunk.

A non-permittee may openly carry a loaded handgun while on foot in most unrestricted public areas. Although not as common as in other open carry states, such carry is legitimate under state statutes and protected from local regulation by Ohio's preemption law.

All Persons: Ohio's licensing law only allows the concealed carry of handguns. Permittees have no special carry privileges with loaded long guns in a vehicle. Such weapons should be transported unloaded and secured in gun cases regardless of one's permit status.

Non-permittees and permittees transporting long guns may carry loaded magazines in the trunk or any container that provides "separate enclosure" for the items. Magazine & gun may be in the same container as long as the magazine is in a separate compartment within that container.

Oklahoma

Total prohibition   *(+3, licensees allowed guns in vehicles on K-12 property)*   **Total freedom**

0 ------ 10 ------ 20 ------ 30 ------ 40 ------ 50 ------ 60 ------ 70 ------ 80 ------ 90 ------ 100

λ

Traveler's checklist:

*   ***Standard firearms ownership:** unrestricted, no permit or license required
*   ***Semi-auto / high capacity magazines:** no restrictions on possession or sale
*   ***Machine gun ownership:** no state restrictions, compliance with federal law only
*   ***Firearm law uniformity:** preemption law, firearm laws uniform throughout state
*   ***Right of Self-Defense:** NRA-model castle doctrine, *stand your ground* in public areas
*   ***Open carry:** generally prohibited in public unless one possesses a valid permit
*   ***Concealed carry:** licenses granted on a "shall issue" basis; automatic recognition of all carry permits; recognition of all persons from "constitutional carry" states
*   ***Vehicle carry by non-permittees:** all firearms must be unloaded and in plain view or secured in visible cases; long guns may be concealed behind the seat
*   ***State Parks:** recognized licensees may carry in open areas, but not in any gov't buildings
*   ***Restaurants serving alcohol:** permittees may carry while eating in dining areas – see p.3
*   ***Duty to notify LEO of permit status:** at the first opportunity upon official contact
*   ***Vehicle gun possession at colleges:** lawful for any gun owner

Oklahoma was opened to pioneer settlement after most of the West had already been "won." Firearms were instrumental in providing these late settlers with a sense of protection as well as self-reliance on the open prairie. Oklahoma's firearm laws reflect much of this tradition.

Recognized permittees/persons: A license is required to carry a loaded handgun. Such permits are issued to residents who are 21 years or older for 5 or 10 year terms. Oklahoma recognizes any permit issued by another state as well as the "right to carry without a permit" for persons residing in states that do not require permits for concealed carry. Such persons should carry their holstered handguns concealed and possess photo IDs that prove their residencies.

Recognized permittees may carry holstered handguns openly or concealed. Carry is limited to handguns that are .45 or less. A recognized permittee/person may transport magazine-loaded long guns anywhere in his vehicle's interior. But when stopped by police, he must inform the officer that he has a handgun at the first opportunity to do so.

Recognized permittees/persons may carry handguns on foot in most public areas. But carry is prohibited in sports arenas, casinos, schools (colleges & K-12), most government bldgs., and posted private businesses. Vehicle gun possession in parking lots for these areas is lawful.

Persons without recognized permits: Handguns possessed within a vehicle must be unloaded and carried in plain view or secured in commercial gun cases that are wholly or partially visible from outside the passenger compartment. Trunk transport of unloaded handguns is also acceptable. Glove compartment or console box carry of a handgun is illegal.

Vehicle carry of rifles and shotguns is allowed as long as the weapons are unloaded. They may be kept in plain view (ie. gun rack) or concealed behind the seat.

Open carry by non-recognized persons while on foot is prohibited in most public areas. Exceptions exist for recreational activities involving guns such as hunting & target shooting.

All Persons: Oklahoma's parking lot storage law prevents property owners from restricting the possession of lawfully owned guns and ammunition in vehicles parked on their lots as long as the firearms are stored in compliance with existing law (ie. unloaded if person is a non-permittee). And Oklahoma prohibits anyone from carrying a firearm aboard a bus.

Oregon

Total prohibition *(+0, no reciprocity & limited preemption keep rating below 80)* **Total freedom**

0 ------ 10 ------ 20 ------ 30 ------ 40 ------ 50 ------ 60 ------ 70 ------ 80 ------ 90 ------ 100

Traveler's checklist:

* **Standard firearms ownership:** unrestricted, no permit or license required
* **Semi-auto gun / high capacity magazines:** no restrictions on possession or sale
* **Machine gun ownership:** no state restrictions, compliance with federal law only
* **Firearm law uniformity:** preemption statute, firearm laws uniform throughout state except for local regulation of loaded firearms carry
* **Right of Self-Defense:** no NRA castle doctrine, *stand your ground* in public not codified
* **Open carry:** unrestricted under state law; some local regulation may exist
* **Concealed carry:** licenses issued to qualified residents on a "shall issue" basis; no reciprocity for travelers with carry permits from other states
* **Vehicle carry by non-permittees:** loaded firearms must be carried in plain view or securely encased in the trunk or storage compartment
* **State Parks:** Oregon permittees may carry concealed handguns
* **Restaurants serving alcohol:** permittees may carry while eating in dining areas – see p.3
* **Duty to notify LEO of permit status:** upon demand of police officer
* **Vehicle gun possession at colleges:** lawful for Oregon permittees only

Oregon's proximity to the highly regulated state of California might cause some to expect gun laws that mirror those of its southern neighbor. While gun carry options for nonresidents could be better, most travelers will find Oregon's timber-rich countryside to be gun-friendly.

Oregon permittees: The state requires a license to carry a concealed handgun on one's person or in a vehicle. The sheriff of a person's home county issues such permits to qualified persons 21 years or older for four year terms. Oregon will only grant licenses to nonresidents who live in a bordering state and express a viable need for concealed carry in Oregon. Such permits are issued at the discretion of any local sheriff. Oregon does not recognize permits to carry firearms issued by other states. An Oregon permittee may carry in most public areas.

Persons without Oregon permits: A loaded handgun may be carried in a vehicle if it is in a visible belt holster. But any handgun that is readily accessible and hidden from view is prohibited. This would include guns kept in unlocked glove compartments, console boxes and under one's seat. Handguns secured in commercial cases and stowed in the trunk are legitimate. If a vehicle has no trunk, a handgun may be kept in a *locked* glove compartment or console box as long as the key is not inserted in the lock. Carrying a concealed handgun in a motorcycle, ATV or snowmobile requires that the gun be either trigger locked or in a locked container.

Long guns may be loaded and carried openly in gun racks. They may also be secured in a closed gun case or vehicle trunk as long as the weapons are not concealed upon the person.

Oregon's preemption law allows localities to regulate the public carry of *loaded* firearms. Portland and other cities require all firearms carried in a public setting or private vehicle to be unloaded and in plain view or securely cased unless the person has an Oregon license. And state law prohibits open carry by non-permittees in any "public building." This would include schools, colleges, hospitals, the state capitol and any local or state government offices.

All Persons: Oregon allows anyone in a recreational vehicle to possess a loaded, concealed handgun without a permit while the RV is parked in a campsite and being utilized as a residence. But RV owners should note that vehicle carry laws apply when they are on the road.

Pennsylvania

Total prohibition *(+3, preemption law better, but unlicensed car carry needs help)* **Total freedom**

0 ------ 10 ------ 20 ------ 30 ------ 40 ------ 50 ------ 60 ------ 70 ------ 80 ------ 90 ------ 100

Traveler's checklist:

*Standard firearms ownership: unrestricted, no permit or license required

*Semi-auto gun / high capacity magazines: no restrictions on possession or sale

*Machine gun ownership: no state restrictions, compliance with federal law only

*Firearm law uniformity: preemption law, firearm laws uniform throughout state

*Right of Self-Defense: NRA-model castle doctrine, *stand your ground* in public areas

*Open carry: unrestricted under state law in most public areas

*Concealed carry: licenses granted on a "shall issue" basis; automatic recognition for vehicle carry of handguns by nonresidents with out-of-state permits

*Vehicle carry by non-permittees: handguns must be unloaded and securely locked in the vehicle trunk or rear storage area; rifles and shotguns must be unloaded and may be in the passenger compartment but should be cased

*State Parks: concealed handgun carry by recognized licensees permitted

*Restaurants serving alcohol: permittees may carry while eating in dining areas – see p.3

*Duty to notify LEO of permit status: upon demand of police officer

*Vehicle gun possession at colleges: subject to college administrative policy

Travelers to Pennsylvania will find the state to have an even mix of urban and rural character. This contributes to a legal dichotomy where gun ownership is both respected and, in certain instances, heavily encumbered. A famous pundit once described Pennsylvania as a state where, "Philadelphia is on one side, Pittsburgh is on the other, and Alabama is in the middle."

Recognized permittees: The state requires a license to carry a loaded handgun in a vehicle or concealed on or about one's person. The sheriff of a resident's home county issues such permits to persons 21 years or older for five year terms. Pennsylvania will also issue permits through any sheriff's office to nonresidents who possess permits from their home states. Any nonresident with a valid, out-of-state permit may carry a loaded handgun in his vehicle so long as he restricts his carry to the vehicle's interior. Concealed carry of a handgun outside one's vehicle is limited to licenses that have been specifically recognized by the Attorney General (see p. 65). Recognized permittees may carry in most public areas except some universally restricted areas (such as K-12 schools)(see p. 6), state capitol grounds and mental hospitals.

Persons without recognized permits: Vehicle carry of any firearm by an unlicensed individual is strictly regulated. Handguns must be unloaded, cased and secured in the trunk or rear storage area. The weapons should also be separated from any ammunition. Travelers should be enroute to a vacation dwelling, gun range or residence unless they have a permit.

Open carry of a loaded handgun while on foot is allowed in most public areas as long as the weapon is secured in a visible belt holster. The state's preemption law prevents localities from regulating any aspect of this carry mode and also provides for legal action against cities that attempt to enforce local ordinances. But travelers should be aware that handgun carry in first class cities such as Philadelphia is limited to someone possessing a valid, recognized license.

All Persons: Rifles and shotguns must be unloaded and should be secured in commercial cases or gun racks. Long guns may be transported in the passenger compartment but should remain unloaded regardless of whether a person possesses a carry permit. Licensed firearms carry only applies to handguns in Pennsylvania.

Rhode Island

Total prohibition *(+0, carry is tough, if not impossible, for most travelers)* **Total freedom**

0 ------ 10 ------ 20 ------ 30 ------ 40 ------ 50 ------ 60 ------ 70 ------ 80 ------ 90 ------ 100

Traveler's checklist:

*   ***Standard firearms ownership:** unrestricted, no permit or license required
*   ***Semi-auto / high capacity magazines:** no restrictions on possession or sale
*   ***Machine gun ownership:** individual possession prohibited
*   ***Firearm law uniformity:** preemption law, firearm laws uniform throughout state
*   ***Right of Self-Defense:** no NRA-model castle doctrine, *duty to retreat* in public areas
*   ***Open carry:** prohibited in all public areas unless one has an attorney general-issued permit
*   ***Concealed carry:** concealed carry permits issued to residents and nonresidents on a discretionary basis; *limited* recognition of out-of-state carry permits
*   ***Vehicle carry by non-permittees:** a carry permit issued by any state or locality is required for transportation of handguns ***through*** the state; unloaded rifles and shotguns may be transported without a permit in a vehicle
*   ***State Parks:** firearms carry prohibited; firearms must be unloaded and cased in vehicle
*   ***Restaurants serving alcohol:** permittees may carry while eating in dining areas – see p.3
*   ***Duty to notify LEO of permit status:** upon demand of police officer
*   ***Vehicle gun possession at colleges:** subject to college administrative policy

Rhode Island's handgun carry laws reflect the restrictive attitude evident along much of the Northeast Coast. Carry is limited to those with enough political influence to acquire a permit. Everyone else must surrender their personal protection rights when they exit the front door.

Recognized permittees: The state requires a license to carry a handgun about his person or in a vehicle. The police chief of an applicant's hometown issues such licenses for a four-year term. Nonresidents with carry permits from other states may apply to any city's police chief for a Rhode Island permit. The attorney general will also issue permits to nonresidents but will not require the possession of another state's permit. Applicants must be at least 21 years or older and be able to articulate a "proper reason" to carry a handgun. This statutory language has prompted some authorities to exercise a certain amount of discretion over permit issuance.

Rhode Island will recognize any carry permit issued by another state or locality if the traveler restricts his transport of the handgun to the interior of his vehicle. He must also be passing through the state on a continuous journey with no intention of staying for any period. This would mean that even a one-day vacation within Rhode Island would not be allowed.

Persons without recognized permits: A person who lacks a permit may only transport a handgun in a vehicle if the weapon is unloaded, secured in a gun case and the ammunition is stowed in the trunk or outside storage compartment. If the vehicle has no trunk, the ammunition must be locked in a separate container. He must also be traveling between his home and business or going to or from a gun shop, gunsmith, repair facility or target range unless he can qualify as a traveler on a "through journey" per p.5.

All Persons: Any person may transport rifles and shotguns in a vehicle as long as the weapons are unloaded. Rhode Island does not require that the firearms be cased or secured in any specific way. But, due to the state's restrictive attitude toward handgun possession, travelers should exercise caution in this area by securing their long guns in commercial gun cases or trunk mounted gun racks. Transport modes such as these will be viewed much more favorably by East Coast police officers not accustomed to firearms carry by citizens.

South Carolina

Total prohibition   *(+3, carry in restaurants serving alcohol, expanded car carry)*   **Total freedom**

0 ------ 10 ------ 20 ------ 30 ------ 40 ------ 50 ------ 60 ------ 70 ------ 80 ------ 90 ------ 100

Traveler's checklist:

*   ***Standard firearms ownership:** unrestricted, no permit or license required
*   ***Semi-auto / high capacity magazines:** no restrictions on possession or sale
*   ***Machine gun ownership:** compliance with relevant portions of federal law
*   ***Firearm law uniformity:** preemption law, firearm laws uniform throughout state
*   ***Right of Self-Defense:** NRA-model castle doctrine, *stand your ground* in public areas
*   ***Open carry:** prohibited in most public areas
*   ***Concealed carry:** licenses granted to qualified persons on a "shall issue" basis; reciprocity for nonresidents with permits from their home states (see p. 65)
*   ***Vehicle carry by non-permittees:** loaded handguns may be carried in a closed glove compartment; rifles and shotguns may be loaded while in the trunk or passenger area (some exceptions - see below)
*   ***State Parks:** concealed handgun carry by recognized licensees permitted
*   ***Restaurants serving alcohol:** permittees may carry while eating in dining areas – see p.3
*   ***Duty to notify LEO of permit status:** immediately upon official contact
*   ***Vehicle gun possession at colleges:** lawful for permittees only

South Carolina's "southern" flavor for firearms is reflected in its laws. A healthy respect for private gun ownership coupled with some very positive jurisprudence ensures a pleasant journey for most while visiting the birthplace of the Confederacy.

Recognized permittees: South Carolina requires a license to carry a concealed handgun on or about one's person. Permits are issued to residents who are at least 21 years old for 5-year terms. A qualified nonresident who owns real property within the state is also eligible for a permit. South Carolina will recognize permits from other states as long as the foreign state requires permittees to pass a criminal background check and firearms safety course. The out-of-state permittee must be a resident of the state where the permit was issued and may only use his permit for *concealed* handgun carry. In a vehicle, this would include on his person, under the seat, or in any open or closed compartment. When approached by a police officer, he must inform the officer that he is carrying a concealed handgun with a permit. Recognized permittees may carry in most areas except scholastic athletic events, medical & day care facilities, govt. meetings, buses, churches and all private businesses & special events that post against carry.

Persons without recognized permits: Vehicle carry of a loaded handgun is allowed if the weapon is contained in a closed glove compartment, console box, or trunk. A motorcycle rider may secure his loaded handgun in a closed saddlebag or similar accessory container.

Handgun carry on foot is restricted to certain specific conditions. Generally, the weapon must be unloaded and secured in a package or closed case. A loaded handgun may be carried from a vehicle to a hotel room so long as its owner has paid the rent and the hotel tax. Licensed hunters and fishermen may also carry loaded handguns while engaged in hunting or fishing.

All Persons: Loaded rifles and shotguns may be carried in a vehicle by anyone unless such carry occurs in a state park, recreational area or wildlife area during hunting season. All long guns must then be unloaded and secured in cases regardless of whether one possesses a license. Also, public buildings, universities and the state capitol are off-limits to any firearm possession unless one is a recognized permittee and his guns remain secured in a locked vehicle.

South Dakota

Total prohibition   *(+0, a great state for gun carry, needs little improvement)*   **Total freedom**

0 ------ 10 ------ 20 ------ 30 ------ 40 ------ 50 ------ 60 ------ 70 ------ 80 ------ 90 ------ 100

$\land$

Traveler's checklist:

- ***Standard firearms ownership:** unrestricted, no permit or license required
- ***Semi-auto / high capacity magazines:** no restrictions on possession or sale
- ***Machine gun ownership:** compliance with applicable federal law
- ***Firearm law uniformity:** preemption law, firearm laws uniform throughout state
- ***Right of Self-Defense:** NRA-model castle doctrine, *stand your ground* in public areas
- ***Open carry:** unrestricted under state law in most public areas
- ***Concealed carry:** licenses granted on a "shall issue" basis; automatic recognition for a non-resident with a carry permit from any other state
- ***Vehicle carry by non-permittees:** handguns may be loaded and carried in plain view or unloaded and carried in the trunk or other closed compartment; loaded rifles and shotguns may be in the passenger area or trunk
- ***State Parks:** concealed handgun carry by recognized licensees permitted
- ***Restaurants serving alcohol:** permittees may carry while eating in dining areas – see p.3
- ***Duty to notify LEO of permit status:** upon demand of police officer
- ***Vehicle gun possession at colleges:** subject to college administrative policy

Travelers to South Dakota will find its firearm laws illustrative of the state's rural character. Permits to carry are readily issued to all qualified applicants and contain few restrictions on where or when a licensee can carry. It's no wonder that President Theodore Roosevelt honed much of his skill with firearms in the Bad Lands of the Mt. Rushmore State.

Recognized permittees: The state requires a license to carry a concealed handgun on one's person or in one's vehicle. Such permits are issued by the Secretary of State through the sheriff of the applicant's home county to qualified residents who are 18 years or older. The permit is issued for a five-year term and allows a person to carry a concealed, loaded handgun in a vehicle as well as concealed on his person. South Dakota only issues licenses to residents but will recognize any out-of-state permit as long as the permittee is a non-resident. Recognized permittees may carry in almost all public areas except bars, courthouses and the state capitol.

Persons without recognized permits: Travelers without recognized permits may carry loaded handguns in a vehicle as long as the weapons are in plain view. A recent Attorney General opinion states that no permit is required to carry a loaded handgun in a vehicle "if any part of the firearm is capable of being seen." Handguns can be hidden from view if they are unloaded and secured in the trunk or other closed compartment. 'Closed compartment' would include the glove compartment or console box. A container specifically designed for transporting a handgun is also acceptable if it is too large for any concealment on one's person.

Open carry of a loaded handgun on foot is permitted under most circumstances and more commonly practiced in the state's rural areas. South Dakota's preemption law prevents localities from regulating most aspects of firearm carry, possession and transport.

All Persons: Vehicle carry of loaded rifles and shotguns is generally unregulated. Such weapons may be carried anywhere including the passenger compartment. But all long guns should be secured in cases when passing through a game preserve or wildlife refuge. Motorcycle and snowmobile riders must unload and case all firearms unless they possess recognized permits. They may then have loaded handguns. But all long guns must remain unloaded and cased.

Tennessee

Total prohibition   *(+9, loaded vehicle carry for non-permittes approved)*   **Total freedom**

0 ------ 10 ------ 20 ------ 30 ------ 40 ------ 50 ------ 60 ------ 70 ------ 80 ------ 90 ------ 100

λ

Traveler's checklist:

*Standard firearms ownership: unrestricted, no permit or license required

*Semi-auto / high capacity magazines: no restrictions on possession or sale

*Machine gun ownership: no state restrictions, compliance with federal law only

*Firearm law uniformity: preemption law, localities may prohibit carry in parks

*Right of Self-Defense: NRA-model castle doctrine, *stand your ground* in public areas

*Open carry: prohibited unless one possesses a recognized permit to carry a handgun

*Concealed carry: licenses granted on a "shall issue" basis; automatic recognition for non-residents with carry permits from any other state

*Vehicle carry by non-permittees: loaded firearms may be carried anywhere in a private motor vehicle (glove compartment, console box, gun case, etc.)

*State Parks: concealed handgun carry by recognized licensees permitted

*Restaurants serving alcohol: permittees may carry while eating in dining areas – see p.3

*Duty to notify LEO of permit status: upon demand of police officer

*Vehicle gun possession at colleges: lawful for permittees, but code enforcement possible

Tennessee has greatly improved its treatment of firearms in recent years. The birthplace of Alvin York has a solid tradition of private gun ownership that should provide most travelers with an enjoyable visit.

Recognized permittees: A license is required to carry a loaded handgun either openly or concealed. Such permits are issued through the Department of Public Safety to qualified residents 21 years or older for 5-year terms. Tennessee recognizes any valid, out-of-state carry permit as long as the permittee is not a resident of Tennessee and restricts his weapons' carry to handguns only. Nonresidents are not issued permits unless they are *regularly employed* in the state. Most areas off-limits to permittee carry, such as colleges, civic centers & public recreation buildings, are posted with signage. These prohibitions can include all property owned by the entity. Although "open areas" such as local parks and campgrounds are O.K. under state law, localities can still prohibit carry in these places by posting signs. Parking lots are exempt from prohibition if the permittee's firearms remain secured from view in a motor vehicle.

Persons without recognized permits: Non-permittees are prohibited from carrying firearms with the "intent to go armed." The actions of the person and the state of the firearms that he has in his possession define this condition. If the weapons are loaded and carried on his person while on foot, he violates the law unless he is engaged in hunting, sport shooting or other gun-related activity. This prevents any open carry of a handgun without a recognized permit.

But a recent law change allows an exception for vehicle carry. Anyone in lawful possession of firearms may carry them loaded anywhere in a motor vehicle. The weapons may be in the glove compartment, console box, trunk, under the seat or secured in commercial gun cases.

All Persons: Tennessee preempts localities from regulating most aspects of the possession, carrying or transportation of firearms and ammunition. But local governments may still prohibit all firearms carry in public parks and "green spaces" by posting signs.

Tennessee's parking lot storage law was recently strengthened to include any vehicle lawfully possessed by a permittee. But, although the law *decriminalizes* firearm possession by permittees, it still allows for policy enforcement by property owners.

Texas

Traveler's checklist:

- ***Standard firearms ownership:** unrestricted, no permit or license required
- ***Semi-auto / high capacity magazines:** no restrictions on possession or sale
- ***Machine gun ownership:** no state restrictions, compliance with federal law only
- ***Firearm law uniformity:** preemption statute, firearm laws uniform throughout state
- ***Right of Self-Defense:** NRA-model castle doctrine, *stand your ground* in public areas
- ***Open carry:** prohibited in all public areas under most circumstances
- ***Concealed carry:** licenses granted on a "shall issue" basis; reciprocity available for carry permits from certain other states (see p.65)
- ***Vehicle carry by non-permittees:** concealed, loaded handguns may be carried anywhere in a vehicle; loaded long guns may be carried anywhere
- ***State Parks:** concealed handgun carry by recognized licensees permitted
- ***Restaurant serving alcohol:** permittees may carry while eating in dining areas – see p.3
- ***Duty to notify LEO of permit status:** immediately upon official contact (ID request)
- ***Vehicle gun possession at colleges:** lawful for permittees and their firearms

Travelers to the Lone Star State will find its reputation as a gun owner's paradise to be rightly deserved. And despite adjusting its frontier laws to fit the demands of a modern society, Texas still embodies the gun loving spirit of native sons Audie Murphy and Sam Houston.

Recognized permittees: The state requires a license to carry a concealed handgun on or about one's person. Such licenses are issued by DPS to residents who are 21 years or older for an initial term of four years and a subsequent renewal term of 5 years. Texas will issue permits to any resident of another state and will recognize permittees from states whose laws mandate background checks of their licensees. A permittee must be at least 21, carry his handgun concealed and inform any policeman who requests his ID that he has a carry license. Places off-limits to carry include bars, racetracks, colleges & sporting events. Hospitals, nursing homes, amusement parks, & churches are off-limits if posted. Parking lots for all these areas are O.K. for licensed carry. And any business may post its property against carry with approved signage.

Persons without recognized permit: A non-permittee may not carry a handgun "on or about his person" while on foot. This would include any readily accessible handgun within arm's reach whether the weapon is concealed or in plain view. Texas exempts persons who are traveling as well as sportsmen involved in lawful firearm activity such as hunting and target shooting. These exemptions apply while a person is actually engaged in these pursuits or enroute between one's home and the area where the exemption is occurring.

Vehicle carry of a loaded handgun is allowed if the weapon is kept concealed and the person carrying the weapon is not involved in any criminal activity (except routine traffic violations). This "traveling presumption" allows anyone, not just those who possess permits, to carry concealed, loaded handguns in their motor vehicles and watercrafts.

All Persons: Loaded long guns may be carried in plain view anywhere in a vehicle or secured in gun cases or window racks. Passenger compartment carry is as lawful as trunk stowage. Local regulation of this and other gun rights is nullified by Texas' preemption law.

Texas also specifies that any recreational vehicle being used as a living quarters is considered one's home where legal prohibitions on loaded handgun carry do not apply.

Utah

Total prohibition *(+2, open carry protected against disorderly conduct charge)* **Total freedom**

0 ------ 10 ------ 20 ------ 30 ------ 40 ------ 50 ------ 60 ------ 70 ------ 80 ------ 90 ------ 100

Traveler's checklist:

* **Standard firearms ownership:** unrestricted, no permit or license required
* **Semi-auto / high capacity magazines:** no restrictions on possession or sale
* **Machine gun ownership:** no state restrictions, compliance with federal law only
* **Firearm law uniformity:** preemption statute, firearm laws uniform throughout state
* **Right of Self-Defense:** NRA-model castle doctrine, *stand your ground* in public areas
* **Open carry:** "loaded" carry by non-permittees prohibited in most public areas (see below)
* **Concealed carry:** licenses granted on a "shall issue" basis; automatic recognition available for carry permits from all other states
* **Vehicle carry by non-permittees:** rifles and shotguns must be unloaded; handguns may be loaded and concealed anywhere in a vehicle
* **State Parks:** concealed handgun carry by recognized licensees permitted
* **Restaurants serving alcohol:** permittees may carry while eating in dining areas – see p.3
* **Duty to notify LEO of permit status:** upon demand of police officer
* **Vehicle gun possession at colleges:** lawful for any gun owner, some code enforcement

Utah was founded more than a century ago by hardy Mormon pioneers who relied heavily upon firearms for survival. Many a battle with Indians and other hostiles was decided by gun-wielding settlers. Modern Utah reflects this frontier heritage in its laws regarding firearms.

Recognized permittees: The state issues a license to carry a concealed firearm on one's person or in a vehicle. The license allows for the carry of any firearm, not just a handgun, and is issued by the Bureau of Criminal Identification to qualified persons 21 years or older for a 5-year term. Utah grants licenses to both residents and non-residents and recognizes any valid, out-of-state carry permit. A recognized permittee may carry a concealed firearm in all public places except secure areas, houses of worship and private residences that post notices. Utah is one of the few states that allow resident permittees to carry in primary & secondary schools.

Persons without recognized permits: Handguns in a vehicle may be loaded and carried openly or concealed from view. A pistol placed under one's seat, in a glove compartment or within a console box is legitimate as long as the vehicle is in the gun owner's lawful possession. The owner must also be eighteen years of age or older.

Utah does not allow the carry of "loaded" firearms on public streets and posted prohibited areas by non-permittees while on foot. But Utah defines "loaded" to only include chamber-loaded semi-autos. So a non-permittee could openly carry a magazine loaded, chamber unloaded pistol and still be O.K. in *most* public areas. Utah preempts local regulation of carry issues.

All Persons: Any traveler, regardless of permit status, may carry long guns in the passenger compartment of his vehicle. Rifles, shotguns and muzzle-loading weapons must remain unloaded. Utah law deems rifles and shotguns to be unloaded when their firing chambers contain no "live" rounds. The weapons' magazines may contain ammunition. Muzzle-loading firearms are loaded when capped or primed. Long guns may be kept in window-mounted gun racks, commercial gun cases or any convenient place for stowage.

Most property owners are prohibited from enforcing "no guns in vehicles" policies in their parking lots if the firearms remain locked in one's vehicle and secured from view. Government entities, churches and schools are exempt from this provision.

Vermont

Total prohibition *(+0, hard to improve perfection, Ethan Allen would be proud!)* **Total freedom**

0 ------ 10 ------ 20 ------ 30 ------ 40 ------ 50 ------ 60 ------ 70 ------ 80 ------ 90 ------ 100

λ

Traveler's checklist:

*   ***Standard firearms ownership:** unrestricted, no permit or license required
*   ***Semi-auto / high capacity magazines:** no restrictions on possession or sale
*   ***Machine gun ownership:** no state restrictions, compliance with federal law only
*   ***Firearm law uniformity:** preemption statute, firearm laws uniform throughout state
*   ***Right of Self-Defense:** no NRA-model castle doctrine
*   ***Open carry:** unrestricted in most public areas and generally accepted
*   ***Concealed carry:** no license required for concealed carry
*   ***Vehicle carry for all persons:** rifles and shotguns carried in a vehicle must be unloaded; handguns may be carried loaded and concealed
*   ***State Parks:** concealed handgun carry by any non-felon permitted
*   ***Restaurants serving alcohol:** any non-felon may carry while eating in dining areas
*   ***Duty to notify LEO of permit status:** N/A – permits not issued by state
*   ***Vehicle gun possession at colleges:** subject to college administrative policy

Vermont's proximity to bastions of gun control along America's East Coast could lead one to expect equally restrictive laws in America's maple syrup capitol. But Vermont is a proudly independent state whose laws reflect the values of its colonial heritage and its rural demographics. Firearms carry of any kind (open or concealed) is properly viewed as a right not subject to regulation. The few laws that do exist should cause little concern for the traveler.

Vermont is one of only four states (the other three being Arizona, Alaska, and Wyoming) that does not require a license to carry a firearm. Persons may carry loaded handguns concealed or openly almost anywhere in the state. Vehicle carry is viewed in the same light as any other carry. A concealed, loaded handgun placed in a glove compartment, console box or briefcase is legitimate. A pistol carried directly on the person is also acceptable. The one qualification is that the weapon may not be carried with the avowed purpose of injuring someone.

Rifles and shotguns in a vehicle may be transported openly or secured in commercial gun cases. But due to hunting and safety considerations, long guns of any type must be unloaded while being transported in a vehicle. Travelers should rely upon a handgun for personal protection while traveling through Vermont.

Vermont prohibits firearm carry in courthouses, schools, and on the grounds of any "state institution." This would generally include facilities such as prisons and mental hospitals as well as most buildings leased or owned by the state government (excluding colleges and universities). Travelers should note this aspect if they intend to carry a firearm while on foot.

Vermont has a preemption law that prevents municipalities from enacting laws that locally regulate the carry, possession or sale of firearms. Cities may still regulate the discharge and use of firearms. But travelers can expect uniformity throughout the state with the firearm laws that most directly affect them.

Virginia

Total prohibition *(+0, the birthplace of presidents is also a great place for guns)* **Total freedom**

0 ------ 10 ------ 20 ------ 30 ------ 40 ------ 50 ------ 60 ------ 70 ------ 80 ------ 90 ------ 100

λ

Traveler's checklist:

*   ***Standard firearms ownership:** unrestricted, no license or permit required
*   ***Semi-auto / high capacity magazines:** "streetsweeper"-style shotguns prohibited – over 20 shot mags prohibited to nonpermittees in certain urban public areas
*   ***Machine gun ownership:** state registration required of machine gun ownership
*   ***Firearm law uniformity:** preemption statute, local units prohibited from regulation
*   ***Right of Self-Defense:** no NRA castle doctrine, *stand your ground* in public not codified
*   ***Open carry:** unrestricted under state law and becoming generally accepted
*   ***Concealed carry:** licenses granted on a "shall issue" basis; reciprocity available for carry permits from certain other states (see p. 65)
*   ***Vehicle carry by non-permittees:** loaded handguns may be carried in plain view or secured in the glove compartment or console box; loaded rifles and shotguns may be kept in gun cases in the passenger compartment or trunk
*   ***State Parks:** concealed handgun carry by recognized licensees permitted
*   ***Restaurants serving alcohol:** permittees may carry while eating in dining areas – see p.3
*   ***Duty to notify LEO of permit status:** upon demand of police officer
*   ***Vehicle gun possession at colleges:** college regulation through VA's administrative code

The birthplace of many of America's founders displays a healthy respect for our constitutional heritage in its laws regulating firearms. Visitors to the Old Dominion will be impressed with how well the state lives up to its historical traditions.

Recognized permittees: Virginia requires a license to carry a handgun concealed about the person and hidden from common observation. Such permits are issued by the circuit court of a person's county of residence for a five-year term and cost $50.00. Virginia will also issue permits to nonresidents through the State Police for a $100.00 fee. Virginia recognizes permits from states whose eligibility standards are similar to Virginia. Recognized permittees must be at least 21 years old and may only carry handguns. Carry is lawful in most public areas except churches (if posted), courthouses, airports, private businesses that ban gun carry and some colleges and universities that regulate carry through Virginia's administrative code.

Persons without recognized permits: A loaded handgun may be carried in a vehicle if the weapon is in plain view or secured in a container or vehicle compartment. "Plain view" would include a holstered handgun on the dashboard or passenger seat. "Vehicle compartment" would include a handgun secured in a glove compartment, console box or trunk. A loaded handgun could also be kept in a briefcase or similar container situated anywhere in the vehicle, including about one's person. Container carry is a blanket exception that includes any position.

Open carry of a loaded handgun on foot is allowed in most public settings. Virginia's preemption law nullifies all existing local ordinances that once regulated this aspect. But the state still prohibits non-permittees from carrying loaded center-fire firearms with magazine capacities of more than 20 rounds in many of Virginia's urban areas.

All Persons: Loaded long gun transport in a vehicle is O.K. in most areas of Virginia if the weapons are in plain view or stowed in the trunk. Long guns must remain unloaded on Dept. of Nat'l Resources property or National Forest lands. The "container" exception for handguns only applies to handguns. Nobody may conceal long guns about their persons.

Washington

Total prohibition   *(+0, good, but unlicensed vehicle carry could be better)*   **Total freedom**

0 ------ 10 ------ 20 ------ 30 ------ 40 ------ 50 ------ 60 ------ 70 ------ 80 ------ 90 ------ 100

Λ

Traveler's checklist:
- ***Standard firearms ownership:** unrestricted, no permit or license required
- ***Semi-auto / high capacity magazines:** no restrictions on possession or sale
- ***Machine gun ownership:** individual ownership prohibited
- ***Firearm law uniformity:** preemption statute, firearm laws uniform throughout state
- ***Right of Self-Defense:** no NRA castle doctrine, *stand your ground* in public not codified
- ***Open carry:** unrestricted under state law in most public areas
- ***Concealed carry:** licenses issued to persons on a "shall issue" basis; reciprocity available for nonresidents with carry permits from certain other states (see p. 65)
- ***Vehicle carry by non-permittees:** handguns must be unloaded and secured in commercial gun cases; long guns must be unloaded
- ***State Parks:** concealed handgun carry by recognized licensees permitted
- ***Restaurants serving alcohol:** permittees may carry while eating in dining areas – see p.3
- ***Duty to notify LEO of permit status:** upon demand of police officer
- ***Vehicle gun possession at colleges:** prohibitions enforced through WA's admin. code

Washington's vast tracts of wilderness create a setting where gun ownership is quite common. Despite being known for left leaning politics (especially near Seattle), the state's gun laws reflect more Rocky Mountain than Pacific coast.

Recognized permittees: The state requires a license to carry a loaded handgun concealed on one's person or in one's vehicle. The police chief of the applicant's hometown issues such permits to residents for five-year terms. Nonresidents may apply in person to any police chief or county sheriff for a license. Washington recognizes permits from states that recognize Washington, require fingerprint-based background checks of their licensees and do not issue permits to persons under 21 years old. A recognized permittee must be a nonresident and may only carry a handgun with his permit. He must also keep the weapon locked up and concealed from view if it is left in his vehicle. Permittees may carry in most public areas except courtrooms, mental health facilities, horse racetracks, outdoor music festivals and many colleges.

Persons without recognized permits: Loaded handguns may not be carried anywhere in a vehicle. Such weapons must be unloaded and secured in gun cases specifically designed for transporting handguns. Loaded magazines may be carried in the passenger compartment as long as they are not inserted into any handgun.

While on foot, a person without a license may carry a loaded, concealed handgun while engaged in outdoor activities such as hunting, fishing, camping, and target shooting. Open carry of a loaded handgun is legitimate as long as the non-permittee secures the weapon in a visible belt holster. Washington's preemption law prevents most local regulation of this carry mode. But cities retain the power to regulate carry by non-permittees in stadiums and convention centers.

All Persons: Rifles and shotguns in a vehicle may be transported in gun racks or cases if the weapons are unloaded. Rifles and shotguns are considered loaded only if the chambers of the weapons are loaded or loaded magazines are attached to the weapons. One may have loaded magazines nearby and still be lawful.

Long guns in vehicles must be unloaded regardless of one's permit status. Carry licenses only authorize loaded handgun carry. And all firearms carried in snowmobiles must be unloaded.

West Virginia

Total prohibition   *(+5, preemption law strengthened, grandfather clause gone)*   **Total freedom**

0 ------ 10 ------ 20 ------ 30 ------ 40 ------ 50 ------ 60 ------ 70 ------ 80 ------ 90 ------ 100

Λ

Traveler's checklist:

*Standard firearms ownership: unrestricted, no permit or license required

*Semi-auto / high capacity magazines: no restrictions on possession or sale

*Machine gun ownership: no state restrictions, compliance with federal law only

*Firearm law uniformity: preemption law, localities prohibited from most regulation; but local restriction still possible in municipally owned bldgs & recreation ctrs.

*Right of Self Defense: NRA-model castle doctrine, *stand your ground* in public areas

*Open carry: unrestricted under state law; some localities may regulate this independently

*Concealed carry: licenses granted to residents on a shall issue basis; reciprocity available for non-residents with permits from certain other states (see p. 65)

*Vehicle carry by non-permittees: firearms should be unloaded and secured in cases

*State Parks: concealed handgun carry by recognized licensees permitted

*Restaurants serving alcohol: permittees may carry while eating in dining areas – see p.3

*Duty to notify LEO of permit status: upon demand of police officer

*Vehicle gun possession at colleges: subject to college administrative policy

West Virginia's independence was exemplified during the Civil War when the state chose to break off from Virginia rather than fight against the Union. Many West Virginians took their privately owned arms to battle, making gun ownership a deeply engrained tradition.

Recognized permittees: The state requires a permit to carry a concealed handgun on one's person or in a vehicle. Sheriffs issue licenses to residents who are at least 21 years of age for five-year terms. West Virginia does not issue permits to nonresidents but will execute agreements with other states for recognition of their permits. The out-of-state permittee must be a non-resident of West Virginia and at least 21 years old for his permit to be valid. A permittee may carry a loaded, concealed handgun in his vehicle or on foot in most public areas. Some local ordinances may prohibit carry in places such as municipal buildings, but areas restricted under state law are generally limited to those listed in the "all persons" section below.

Persons without recognized permits: A non-permittee may not transport loaded or concealed firearms in a vehicle. "Concealed" would include any deadly weapon carried on or about one's person and hidden from ordinary observation. Some sources have suggested that firearms not used in hunting (such as defensive handguns) could be carried loaded and in plain view and still be legitimate under the law. But because current statutes covering this area fail to provide any clear definitional distinction between "hunting" and "defensive" firearms, the state police recommend that non-permittees unload and case all firearms so that the weapons are not readily accessible. Any ammunition should be stored separately.

Open carry of a firearm on foot is allowed in most public areas that are not restricted by local ordinance. The state's preemption law still allows cities to restrict open carry on municipal property by posting signs. But parking lot storage is O.K. if the weapon remains out of view.

All Persons: Shotguns and rifles kept in vehicles should remain unloaded for everyone, even recognized permittees. Permittees are not authorized to carry loaded long guns. And West Virginia's hunting laws regulating long guns are broad enough to cover all persons. Along with most universally restricted areas, carry is prohibited to anyone in courthouses, schools (including vocational schools), the state capitol and any private or city property posting signs against carry.

Wisconsin

Total prohibition *(+0, great improvements, some minor tweaking required)* **Total freedom**

0 ------ 10 ------ 20 ------ 30 ------ 40 ------ 50 ------ 60 ------ 70 ------ 80 ------ 90 ------ 100

Traveler's checklist:

- ***Standard firearms ownership:** unrestricted, no permit or license required
- ***Semi-auto / high capacity magazines:** no restrictions on possession or sale
- ***Machine gun ownership:** approval of sheriff and compliance with federal law
- ***Firearm law uniformity:** preemption statute, firearm laws uniform throughout state
- ***Right of Self-Defense:** NRA-model castle doctrine, *stand your ground* in vehicle only
- ***Open carry:** unrestricted under state law and affirmed by statute and A.G. opinion
- ***Concealed carry:** licenses issued to residents on a shall issue basis; recognition of nonresidents with permits from certain other states (see p. 65)
- ***Vehicle carry by non-permittees:** handguns may be loaded; long guns must be unloaded; no firearms may be concealed (see below)
- ***State Parks:** concealed handgun carry by recognized licensees permitted
- ***Restaurants serving alcohol:** permittees may carry while eating in dining areas – see p.3
- ***Duty to notify LEO of permit status:** upon demand of police officer
- ***Vehicle gun possession at colleges:** lawful for any gun owner

Sportsmen visiting Wisconsin will enjoy the numerous wildlife areas set aside for hunting and fishing activities while tourists will find the temperate climate quite refreshing. With the recent passage of its new carry law, Wisconsin has become a very friendly place for gun owners.

Recognized permittees: Wisconsin requires a license issued by the state's Department of Justice to carry a concealed, loaded handgun. Such licenses are valid for five years and are only issued to Wisconsin residents who are at least 21 years of age. Wisconsin will recognize carry permits from states that perform background checks on their licensees as long as the licensee is 21 years or older, not a Wisconsin resident and has a photo ID. A permittee may carry a handgun, either openly or concealed, in most public areas except mental health facilities, courthouses and secure areas. Colleges, local governments, special event promoters and most private businesses may post against carry within their buildings. But parking lot facilities in these areas, and dorm rooms in colleges, are exempt from such prohibitions. Employers are also prohibited from banning gun possession in employee-owned cars parked on their lots.

Persons without recognized permits: Loaded handguns may not be concealed in any motor vehicle (includes ATVs and boats). Wisconsin courts have developed a strict definition of what constitutes "concealed." Even having a gun on your front seat is prohibited. So, despite amending its law to allow handguns to be uncased and loaded, Wisconsin continues to restrict "open carry" in vehicles. Non-permittees with loaded handguns should keep the weapons stowed in the trunk or rear storage area where they are not within anyone's immediate reach.

Open carry on foot is allowed in most public areas as long as the handgun is in a visible belt holster. Wisconsin affirmed the right of open carry by statute. Police are now prohibited from using disorderly conduct ordinances to arrest someone who is openly carrying a handgun.

All Persons: Longs guns in a vehicle must be unloaded and should be stowed in the trunk or rear storage area. Unloaded is when the chambers or attached magazines contain no ammunition. Loaded, unattached magazines may be kept anywhere in the vehicle. This recommendation pertains to both licensees and non-licensees since Wisconsin's new carry law does not apply to the possession of long guns.

Wyoming

0 ------ 10 ------ 20 ------ 30 ------ 40 ------ 50 ------ 60 ------ 70 ------ 80 ------ 90 ------ 100

Λ

Traveler's checklist:

*   ***Standard firearms ownership:** unrestricted, no permit or license required
*   ***Semi-auto gun / high capacity magazines:** no restrictions on possession or sale
*   ***Machine gun ownership:** no state restrictions, compliance with federal law only
*   ***Firearm law uniformity:** preemption law, firearm laws uniform throughout the state
*   ***Right of Self-Defense:** NRA castle doctrine, *stand your ground* in public not codified
*   ***Open carry:** unrestricted in most public areas and generally accepted
*   ***Concealed carry:** licenses granted on a "shall issue" basis; reciprocity available for concealed carry licenses from certain other states (see p. 65)
*   ***Vehicle carry by non-permittees:** non-residents may carry loaded firearms in plain view or secured in gun cases anywhere in the vehicle; residents who are 21 years or older may carry loaded firearms concealed anywhere in the vehicle
*   ***State Parks:** concealed handgun carry by recognized licensees permitted
*   ***Restaurants serving alcohol:** permittees may carry while eating in dining areas – see p.3
*   ***Duty to notify LEO of permit status:** upon demand of police officer
*   ***Vehicle gun possession at colleges:** subject to college administrative policy

The "Cowboy State" recently joined Arizona, Vermont and Alaska as one of four states to legislate constitutional carry. Although Wyoming limits this right to residents only, the implementation of such law serves to further enhance the state's pro-gun reputation.

Recognized permittees: Wyoming issues a license to carry a concealed handgun on one's person. Such permits are issued by the Attorney General through the sheriff of an applicant's home county for five year terms to qualified residents 21 years or older. The state does not grant permits to nonresidents but will recognize permits from other states so long as they recognize Wyoming permits and issue licenses through a state agency. Recognized permittees can carry concealed handguns in most public places except athletic events, schools (including colleges and universities), churches, bars, courthouses, legislative meetings and the state capitol.

Persons without recognized permits: A non-resident may carry a loaded handgun in a vehicle if the weapon is in plain view. This would include handguns in visible belt holsters or displayed on the vehicle's dashboard or passenger seat. Wyoming only prohibits the "wearing or carrying" of a concealed weapon. So a handgun not worn or carried by the person may be secured in a commercial gun case, glove compartment, or other closed container.

A non-resident may also openly carry a handgun while on foot. The weapon must be visible to casual observation and should be secured in a snapped belt holster. Wyoming's preemption law prevents localities from regulating any aspect of this carry mode.

Any person who has been a resident of Wyoming for at least six months, is 21 years or older and has no disqualifying criminal past may carry a concealed firearm without a permit. He is still under the same carry restrictions as permittees. But his concealed carry requires no permit.

All Persons: Non-residents may transport loaded long guns in gun racks or commercial gun cases. Long guns may not be concealed on the person even if one possesses a recognized permit. Wyoming only authorizes concealed *handgun* carry with a license. But Wyoming residents who fit the above qualifications may transport long guns anywhere in a vehicle.

Travel to Canada and Mexico

Despite a common language and a somewhat similar heritage, Canada's legal treatment of firearms is a shocking reminder of just how different America's neighbor to the North remains. Canada prohibits the importation of any handgun without an Authorization to Transport (ATT). These ATTs are rarely issued to Americans and are given to Canadians on a highly discretionary basis. Travelers without an ATT who attempt to enter Canada with handguns will have their weapons confiscated, their vehicles impounded and could face prosecution. Securely casing the handgun and stowing it in the trunk will not prevent seizure. Mere possession of a handgun anywhere in a vehicle without an ATT is illegal.

Most semi-automatic military pattern firearms are also prohibited from importation. The Canadian parliament enacted a series of draconian gun laws that effectively ban almost every weapon that looks even remotely military. M1 Garands and certain AR-15 rifles are exempt from this general prohibition. M1s are treated like standard sporting rifles and AR-15s are subject to the same restrictions as handguns. But the importation of most military pattern weapons as well as any Class III firearms (machine guns, short barreled rifles and short barreled shotguns) is strictly prohibited. And over 5 shot magazines for center-fire long guns as well as over 10 shot magazines for center-fire pistols are banned from entering the country.

Most individuals may only bring those rifles and shotguns classified as "sporting" into the country. Sporting weapons are defined as "regular sporting rifles or shotguns with barrels over 18.5 inches and longer than 26 inches in overall length." A <u>Non-Resident Firearms Declaration Form</u> is now required for importation. Such forms must be completed in triplicate before a traveler reaches the Canadian border but should not be signed until arriving at the port of entry. These permits cost $25.00 and are valid for 60 days. Travelers should contact Canadian authorities at **204-983-3500** to receive copies of these forms.

Upon reaching the border, you should have your firearm unloaded and separate from any ammunition. The weapon should also be secured in a gun case that is kept out of sight or securely locked in the trunk. A secure locking device, such as a trigger or cable lock, can also be used to secure the firearm. If asked by Customs for a reason why you are transporting a firearm into the country, the traveler should respond that he intends to engage in hunting or officially-sanctioned target competition. Personal defense is not a reason for firearm possession in Canada.

Upon returning to the U.S., you should have proof that the firearms you took into Canada are yours and that you are not importing new firearms into the country. Customs officials recommend a purchase receipt, bill of sale, household inventory list, packing list or a Customs Form 4457 completed prior to your trip. Some customs officials will also accept the Canadian "firearms declaration form" as proof that you owned the gun prior to entering Canada.

Travel to Mexico with firearms is not recommended. Possession of most firearms as well as ammunition is illegal. As Marine Sgt. Andrew Tahmooressi found to his horror, travelers who visit Mexico with firearms are arrested and forced to languish in prison until the intervention of U.S. authorities secures their release. Mexican law presumes your guilt. In other words, once you are arrested, you are guilty until proven innocent. Special permits may be obtained to bring hunting rifles into the country. Contact the Mexican consulate for information at **(202) 736-1000.**

Contact Agencies

Attorney General of Alabama
P.O. Box 300152
Montgomery, AL 36130
(334) 242-7300
www.ago.alabama.gov

Alaskan State Police
5700 E. Tudor Road
Anchorage, AK 99507
(907) 269-0392
www.dps.alaska.gov

Arizona Department of Public Safety
P.O. Box 6488
Phoenix, AZ 85005
(602) 256-6280
www.azdps.gov

Arkansas State Police Headquarters
1 State Police Plaza Drive
Little Rock, AR 72209
(501) 618-8000
www.asp.state.ar.us

California Bureau of Firearms
P.O. Box 820200
Sacramento, California 94203 0200
(916) 227-7527
www.oag.ca.gov

Colorado Bureau of Investigation
P.O. Box 280629
Denver, CO 80228
(303) 813 5700
www.colorado.gov/cbi

Connecticut Department of Public Safety
1111 Country Club Road
Middletown, CT 06457
(860) 685-8190
www.ct.gov/despp

Attorney General of Delaware
820 North French Street
Wilmington, DE 19801
(302) 577-8600
www.attorneygeneral.delaware.gov

Washington Metropolitan Police Dept.
300 Indiana Avenue NW – 5th Floor
Washington D.C. 20001
(202) 727-9099
www.mpdc.dc.gov

Florida Bureau of License Issuance
P.O. Box 6687
Tallahassee, FL 32314 6687
(850) 245-5691
www.freshfromflorida.com

Attorney General of Georgia
40 Capitol Square, SW
Atlanta, GA 30334
(404) 656-3300
www.law.ga.gov

Attorney General of Hawaii
425 Queen Street
Honolulu, HI 96813
(808) 586-1500
www.ag.hawaii.gov

Attorney General of Idaho
P.O. Box 83720
Boise, ID 83720
(208) 334-2400
www.ag.idaho.gov

Illinois State Police
801 S. 7th St.
Springfield, IL 62703
(217) 782-7980
www.isp.state.il.us

Indiana State Police
100 N. Senate Avenue / IGCN
Indianapolis, IN 46204
(317) 232-8264
www.in.gov/isp

Attorney General of Iowa
1305 E. Walnut, Hoover Building
Des Moines, IA 50319
(515) 281-5164
www.state.ia.us/government/ag

Attorney General of Kansas
120 SW Tenth Avenue – 2nd Floor
Topeka, KS 66612-1597
(785) 291-3765
www.ag.ks.gov

Louisiana State Police / CHP Section
P.O. Box 66375
Baton Rouge, LA 70896-6375
(225) 925-4867
www.lsp.org

Attorney General of Maryland
200 Saint Paul Place
Baltimore, MD 21202
(410) 576-6300
www.oag.state.md.us

Michigan State Police
P.O. Box 30634
Lansing, MI 48909
(517) 332-2521
www.michigan.gov/msp

Mississippi Highway Patrol / Gun Permits
P.O. Box 958
Jackson, MS 39205-0958
(601) 987-1212
www.dps.state.ms.us

Attorney General of Montana
215 North Sanders / P.O. Box 201401
Helena, MT 59620-1401
(406) 444-2026
www.dojmt.gov

Nevada Department of Public Safety
555 Wright Way
Carson City, NV 89711-0900
(775) 684-4808
www.dps.nv.gov

New Jersey State Police
P.O. Box 7068
W. Trenton, NJ 08628
(609) 882-2000
www.njsp.org

New York State Police
1220 Washington Ave., Bldg. 22
Albany, NY 12226
(518) 783-3211
www.troopers.ny.gov

Kentucky State Police / Legal Affairs
919 Versailles Road
Frankfort, KY 40601
(502) 782-1800
www.Kentuckystatepolice.org

Maine Department of Public Safety
45 Commerce / State House 164
Augusta, ME 04333
(207) 624-7210
www.maine.gov/dps

Firearms Bureau of Massachusetts
200 Arlington Street, Ste. 220
Chelsea, MA 02150
(617) 660-4782
www.mass.gov/eopss

Minnesota Dept. of Public Safety
445 Minnesota St.
St. Paul, MN 55101
(651) 215 1328
www.dps.mn.gov

Attorney General of Missouri
207 West High Street, P.O. Box 899
Jefferson City, MO 65102
(573) 751-3321
www.ago.mo.gov

Nebraska State Police
P.O. Box 94907
Lincoln, NE 68509
(402) 471-4545
www.statepatrol.nebraska.gov

New Hampshire State Police
33 Hazen Drive
Concord, NH 03305
(603) 223-3873
www.nh.gov/safety

New Mexico Dept. of Public Safety
6301 Indian School Rd. NE - #310
Albuquerque, NM 87110
(505) 841-8053
www.dps.state.nm.us

Attorney General of North Carolina
9001 Mail Service Center
Raleigh, NC 27699-9001
(919) 716-6400
www.ncdoj.com

Attorney General of North Dakota
Dept. 125 / 600 East Boulevard Avenue
Bismarck, ND 58505
(701) 328-2210
www.ag.nd.gov

Oklahoma Bureau of Investigation
6600 N. Harvey
Oklahoma City, Oklahoma 73116
(405) 848-6724
www.ok.gov/osbi

Attorney General of Pennsylvania
16th Floor / Strawberry Square
Harrisburg, PA 17120
(717) 787-3391
www.attorneygeneral.gov

South Carolina Law Enforcement Division
P.O. Box 21398
Columbia, SC 29221
(803) 896-7015
www.sled.sc.gov

Tennessee Department of Public Safety
P.O. Box 945
Nashville, TN 37202
(615) 251-8590
www.tn.gov/safety

Utah Department of Public Safety
3888 West 5400 South
Salt Lake City, UT 84129
(801) 965-4445
www.publicsafety.utah.gov

Virginia State Police
P.O. Box 27472
Richmond, VA 23261 7472
(804) 674-2000
www.vsp.state.va.us

Attorney General of West Virginia
State Capitol Bldg. 1, Room 26E
Charleston, WV 25305
(304) 558-2021
www.ago.wv.gov

Attorney General of Wyoming / DCI
208 S. College Dr.
Cheyenne, WY 82002
(307) 777-7181
www.wyomingdci.wyo.gov

Attorney General of Ohio
30 East Broad Street - 14th Floor
Columbus, OH 43215 3428
(800) 282-0515
www.ohioattorneygeneral.gov

Attorney General of Oregon
1162 Court Street NE
Salem, OR 97301
(503) 378-4400
www.doj.state.or.us

Attorney General of Rhode Island
150 S. Main Street
Providence, RI 02903
(401) 274-4400
www.riag.ri.gov

South Dakota Secretary of State
500 East Capitol Avenue / Ste. 204
Pierre, SD 57501-5070
(605) 773-3537
www.sdsos.gov

Texas Department of Public Safety
P.O. Box 4087
Austin, TX 78773
(512) 424-7293
www.txdps.state.tx.us

Attorney General of Vermont
109 State Street
Montpelier, VT 05609-1001
(802) 828-3171
www.atg.state.vt.us

Attorney General of Washington
P.O. Box 40100
Olympia, WA 98504
(360) 753-6200
www.atg.wa.gov

Attorney General of Wisconsin
P.O. Box 7857
Madison, WI 53707
(608) 266-1221
www.doj.state.wi.us

Royal Canadian Mounted Police
Canadian Firearms Program
Ottawa, Ontario K1A 0R2
(204) 983 3500
www.rcmp.gc.ca

Reciprocity & Recognition

The list below is based on information received from the various state agencies charged with formulating reciprocity lists. Unlike states such as <u>Alabama</u>, **Arizona**, **Arkansas**, **Alaska**, **Idaho**, <u>**Indiana**</u>, <u>**Iowa**</u>, <u>**Kansas**</u>, <u>**Kentucky**</u>, **Michigan***, **Mississippi**, **Missouri**, **North Carolina**, **Oklahoma**, <u>**South Dakota**</u>, <u>**Tennessee**</u>, **Utah & Vermont** which extend automatic recognition to all other states, the following states have reciprocity lists which are based on decisions by state administrators. Their interpretations of reciprocity statutes determine which states they choose to recognize and which states they choose not to recognize. As always, any bureaucratic decision is subject to change. Travelers should contact these states before traveling to them to verify the status of their permits. The information below is confirmed as of December 1, 2014. States not listed below or in this paragraph **do not** recognize **any** out-of-state permits.

*States with this star only recognize permittees who are residents of the state where the permit was issued.

States that are <u>UNDERLINED</u> will not recognize out-of-state permits held by their residents.

<u>**Colorado***</u>   *recognizes permits from*   Alabama, Alaska, Arizona, Arkansas, Delaware, Florida, Georgia, Idaho, Indiana, Iowa, Kansas, Kentucky, Louisiana, Michigan, Mississippi, Missouri, Montana, Nebraska, New Hampshire, New Mexico, North Carolina, North Dakota, Oklahoma, Pennsylvania, South Dakota, Tennessee, Texas, Utah, West Virginia, Wisconsin, Wyoming

<u>**Delaware**</u>   *recognizes permits from*   Alaska, Arizona, Arkansas, Colorado, Florida, Kentucky, Maine, Michigan, Missouri, North Carolina, North Dakota, Ohio, Oklahoma, Tennessee, Texas, Utah, West Virginia

<u>**Florida***</u>   *recognizes permits from*   Alabama, Alaska, Arizona, Arkansas, Colorado, Delaware, Georgia, Idaho, Indiana, Iowa, Kansas, Kentucky, Louisiana, Michigan, Mississippi, Missouri, Montana, Nebraska, New Hampshire, New Mexico, North Carolina, North Dakota, Ohio, Oklahoma, Pennsylvania, South Carolina, South Dakota, Tennessee, Texas, Utah, Virginia, West Virginia, Wyoming

<u>**Georgia**</u>   *recognizes permits from*   Alabama, Alaska, Arizona, Arkansas, Colorado, Florida, Idaho, Indiana, Iowa, Kansas, Kentucky, Louisiana, Michigan, Mississippi, Missouri, Montana, New Hampshire, North Carolina, North Dakota, Oklahoma, Pennsylvania, South Dakota, Tennessee, Texas, Utah, West Virginia, Wisconsin, Wyoming

<u>**Louisiana**</u>   *recognizes permits from*   Alabama, Alaska, Arizona, Arkansas, Colorado, Florida, Georgia, Idaho, Indiana, Iowa, Kansas, Kentucky, Maine, Michigan, Minnesota, Mississippi, Missouri, Montana, Nebraska, New Hampshire, North Carolina, North Dakota, Ohio, Oklahoma, Pennsylvania, South Carolina, South Dakota, Tennessee, Texas, Utah, Virginia, Washington, West Virginia, Wisconsin, Wyoming

<u>**Maine***</u>   *recognizes permits from*   Arkansas, Delaware, Louisiana, Michigan, North Dakota, Pennsylvania, South Dakota, Wyoming

Minnesota *recognizes permits from* Alaska, Arkansas, Kansas, Kentucky, Louisiana, Michigan, Missouri, Nevada, New Mexico, Ohio, Oklahoma, Tennessee, Texas, Utah, Wyoming

Montana *recognizes permits from* **ALL STATES** that issue permits **EXCEPT** Delaware, Hawaii, Maine, New Hampshire, Rhode Island, District of Columbia

Nebraska *recognizes permits from* **ALL STATES** that issue permits **EXCEPT** Alabama, Delaware, Georgia, Indiana, Maryland, Massachusetts, Mississippi, New Hampshire, New York, Pennsylvania, South Dakota, Washington

Nevada *recognizes permits from* Alaska, Arkansas, Idaho (enhanced permits only), Illinois, Kansas, Kentucky, Michigan, Nebraska, New Mexico, North Carolina, Ohio, North Dakota, South Carolina, Tennessee

New Hampshire* *recog. permits from* Alabama, Arizona, Arkansas, Colorado, Florida, Georgia, Idaho, Indiana, Iowa, Kentucky, Louisiana, Michigan, Missouri, Mississippi, North Carolina, North Dakota, Oklahoma, Pennsylvania, Tennessee, Utah, West Virginia, Wyoming

New Mexico *recognizes permit from* Alaska, Arizona, Arkansas, Colorado, Delaware, Idaho (enhanced permits only), Florida, Kansas, Louisiana, Michigan, Mississippi, Missouri, Nebraska, Nevada, North Carolina, North Dakota, Ohio, Oklahoma, South Carolina, Tennessee, Texas, Virginia, West Virginia, Wyoming

North Dakota *recognizes permits from* Alabama, Alaska, Arizona, Arkansas, Colorado, Delaware, Florida, Georgia, Idaho, Indiana, Iowa, Kansas, Kentucky, Louisiana, Maine, Michigan, Mississippi, Missouri, Montana, Nebraska, Nevada, New Hampshire, New Mexico, North Carolina, Ohio, Oklahoma, Pennsylvania, South Carolina, South Dakota, Tennessee, Texas, Utah, Virginia, Washington, West Virginia, Wisconsin, Wyoming

Ohio *recognizes permits from* Alaska, Arizona, Arkansas, Delaware, Florida, Idaho, Kansas, Kentucky, Louisiana, Michigan, Missouri, Nebraska, New Mexico, North Carolina, North Dakota, Oklahoma, South Carolina, Tennessee, Utah, Virginia, Washington, West Virginia, Wyoming

Pennsylvania *recognizes permits from* Alaska, Arizona (resident permits only), Arkansas, Colorado, Georgia, Florida (resident permits only), Indiana, Iowa, Kansas, Kentucky, Louisiana, Maine (resident permits only), Michigan, Missouri, Mississippi (resident permits only), Montana, New Hampshire, North Carolina, North Dakota, Oklahoma, South Dakota, Tennessee, Texas, Utah (resident permits only), Virginia (resident permits only), West Virginia (resident permits only), Wisconsin, Wyoming

South Carolina* *recog. permits from* Alaska, Arizona, Arkansas, Florida, Idaho (enhanced permits only), Kansas, Kentucky, Louisiana, Michigan, Missouri, New Mexico, North Carolina, North Dakota, Ohio, Oklahoma, Texas, Tennessee, Virginia, West Virginia, Wyoming

Texas *recognizes permits from* **ALL STATES** that issue permits **EXCEPT** District of Columbia, Illinois, Maine, Minnesota, New Hampshire, Ohio, Oregon, Wisconsin

Virginia *recognizes permits from* Alaska, Arizona, Arkansas, Delaware, Florida, Idaho (enhanced permits only), Indiana, Kansas, Kentucky, Louisiana, Michigan, Minnesota, Mississippi, Montana, Nebraska, New Mexico, North Carolina, North Dakota, Ohio, Oklahoma, Pennsylvania, South Carolina, South Dakota, Tennessee, Texas, Utah, Washington, Wisconsin, West Virginia, Wyoming

Washington *recognizes permits from* Arkansas, Idaho (enhanced permits only), Kansas, Louisiana, Michigan, Mississippi, Missouri, North Carolina, North Dakota, Ohio, Oklahoma, Tennessee, Utah

West Virginia *recognizes permits from* Alabama, Alaska, Arizona, Arkansas, Colorado, Delaware, Florida, Georgia, Idaho, Iowa, Kansas, Kentucky, Louisiana, Michigan, Mississippi, Missouri, Nebraska, New Hampshire, New Mexico, North Carolina, North Dakota, Ohio, Oklahoma, Pennsylvania, South Carolina, South Dakota, Tennessee, Texas, Utah, Virginia, Wyoming

Wisconsin *recognizes permit from* Alaska (only permits issued after 1/14/13), Arizona, Arkansas, California, Colorado, Connecticut, Georgia, Hawaii, Idaho, Illinois, Indiana, Iowa, Kansas, Kentucky, Louisiana, Maryland, Michigan, Minnesota, Montana, Missouri (only permits issued after 8/28/13), Nebraska, Nevada (only permits issued after 7/1/11), New Mexico, New York, North Carolina, North Dakota, Pennsylvania, Tennessee, Texas, Utah, Virginia (non-resident permits only), West Virginia (only permits issued after 6/8/12), Washington, Wyoming, Puerto Rico, U.S. Virgin Islands

Wyoming *recognizes permits from* Alabama, Alaska, Arizona, Arkansas, Colorado, Florida, Georgia, Idaho, Indiana, Iowa, Kansas, Kentucky, Louisiana, Maine, Michigan, Minnesota, Mississippi, Missouri, Montana, Nebraska, New Hampshire, New Mexico, North Carolina, North Dakota, Ohio, Oklahoma, Pennsylvania, South Carolina, South Dakota, Tennessee, Texas, Utah, Virginia, West Virginia, Wisconsin

---

North Dakota issues Class 1 and Class 2 licenses. This list encompasses recognition of Class 1 licenses only.

Readers may notice occasional inconsistencies with the information presented in the above lists. For example, a state that requires another state to recognize its permits before it will recognize the other state's permits may show recognition for a state that does not include the former state on its list. This is not an editor's error. These lists are taken from official sources at time of printing and may be subject to bureaucratic error. Readers are encouraged to contact the state that appears to be in error to acquire more information regarding recognition of the permit in question.

Although states generally add, rather than delete, states from their lists, deletions during midyear do occasionally occur. Nevada has been known to do this more frequently than other states. Travelers should contact a state's official agency before traveling if news of such deletions are reported in the media.

Traveler's Guide to the Firearm Laws of the Fifty States

Traveler's Guide
P.O. Box 2156
Covington, Kentucky 41012
Phone: (859) 491-6400 (M-F 10a.m. - 5p.m. ET) or Fax: (859) 491-5400 (24 hrs./ 7 days)
www.gunlawguide.com

Dear Customer:

Thank you for purchasing the **Traveler's Guide to the Firearm Laws of the Fifty States.** We hope you will find the information contained in the book to be helpful in your travels with firearms. Credit card customers should note that their purchases will be charged on their statements to *Gunlaw Guide for 50 States.* If you should wish to order additional books, the following is a pro-rated pricing guide for quantity orders:

Qty.	Discount	Pricing
1-4 books	no shipping charge	$14.95 each
5-9 books	less 20% (no S&H)	$11.95 each
10-24 books	less 35% + $8.00 S&H	$9.72 each
25-49 books	less 45% + $14.00 S&H	$8.22 each
50 + books	less 50% + $20.00 S&H	$7.47 each

Payment Terms:

1.) Payment in advance / COD available on quantities of 50 or more
2.) Credit Card, check or money order made out to "Traveler's Guide"

*********************************Order Form*******************************

Name _____

Address (Street)_____

Address (City, State and Zip)_____

Phone:_____E-mail:_____

Quantity_____ Amount enclosed (check or money order)_____

(Dis., Visa, MC) _ _ _ _ - _ _ _ _ - _ _ _ _ - _ _ _ _ Exp.____Security Code _ _ _

Signature of card holders_____